PROPERTY OF
ARAB PUBLIC LIBRARY

J   20021283
624.1775   MacGregor, Anne,
MAC   Domes, a project book

Domes, A Project Book

It is unlawful for any
person to fail to return
library materials.

Domes
A Project Book

With thanks to Maria Fasano,
the Majordomo

Domes
tells the story of these fascinating structures
from the very beginning to the present day.
The dome story comes alive through the
pages of this fully illustrated book,
which features detailed drawings of the
world's most important domes and clear
instructions for the construction of two dome
models. Using everyday materials to make
dome structures, the models—a mosque and a
geodesic dome—are put together using real
architectural and engineering principles in a
simple and creative way. With technical
jargon translated into layman's terms, this
book makes interesting reading for children
and parents alike.

Domes
A Project Book

Anne and Scott MacGregor

Lothrop, Lee & Shepard Books • New York

Designed by Nick Thirkell Associates

The authors wish to thank the following institutions for their assistance with information materials: the New York Public Library and the Instituto Italiano di Cultura.

Text and illustrations copyright © 1981
by Anne and Scott MacGregor
First published in Great Britain in 1981 by Pepper Press, an imprint of E.J. Arnold & Son Ltd.
All rights reserved. No part of this book may be reproduced or utilized in any form or by any means electronic or mechanical, including photocopying, recording or by any information storage and retrieval system, without permission in writing from the Publisher. Inquiries should be addressed to Lothrop, Lee & Shepard Books, a division of William Morrow & Company, Inc., 105 Madison Avenue, New York, New York 10016.
Printed in the United States of America.
First U.S. Edition
1 2 3 4 5 6 7 8 9 10

Library of Congress Cataloging in Publication Data
MacGregor, Anne, (date)
Domes, a project book.
Summary: Explains the history, meaning, and structure of domes, elaborating on particular types such as circles on squares, domes within domes, and modern domes, which include the geodesic. Provides instructions for building model domes.
1. Domes—Juvenile literature. [1. Domes]
I. MacGregor, Scott (date). II. Title.
TH2170.M3   624.1′775   81-11782
ISBN 0-688-00869-0 (lib. bdg.)   AACR2
ISBN 0-688-00870-4 (pbk.)

Contents

I	Domes: An Early History	7
II	Understanding the Meaning and the Structure	13
III	Circles on Squares	23
IV	Domes Within Domes	35
V	The Modern Dome	43

I Domes: An Early History

There are many theories about the origin of domes, but because there are hardly any traces left of the earliest of these structures, we can only guess at how and why they were first developed.

One theory, which seems quite logical, has to do with clay pots. Pots were made by man before free-standing shelters were constructed. There is evidence to prove that clay pots, some quite large, were made around 7000 B.C. in Asia in the region now known as the Middle East. Earthenware pots, as pictured here, were used to store oil, wine, grain, dried fruit, and any other foodstuffs that were kept in bulk. Sometimes these same pots were used as tombs for the dead.

Ancient shelters looked very much like these storage pots, as village houses built by remote tribal people do today. Man's experience in working with clay to form everyday utensils seems to have led to its use in the construction of domed buildings. There is clearly a resemblance between the shapes and materials used.

Different Materials

Early domes, however, were not always built of clay. Some were made of wood poles lashed together and thatched with palms, grasses, or reeds; some, such as the dome-shaped tent, had a wood frame covered with fabric. There were even domes made of snow—the Eskimo's igloo—which are still being built today.

Though each of these structures used very different materials, they were all domes. Many of the construction principles and ideas that went into making them have survived thousands of years, enabling people to build the grand cathedrals of the Renaissance as well as the high-technology geodesic domes of today.

In parts of Africa, rural people build their villages near a source of water, particularly areas surrounding fertile river basins. Here food crops prosper, livestock have food, water, and land on which to graze, and hunting is good.

In such areas, building materials are plentiful and readily available. The soil, a combination of clay and sand, is easy to handle and can be a long-lasting building material if properly cared for. It can also be made into practically any building shape, which makes it very suitable for dome construction.

South of Lake Chad in Africa, small communities live in compact villages like the one pictured here. Domed houses and granaries, or food storehouses, are built close together and connected by a wall that forms a *kraal*, or courtyard. Livestock can be herded into the kraal. All buildings are made of

clay bricks, strengthened with pebbles and straw, and baked in the sun.

Rows of clay bricks known as *courses* are laid from the ground up. Each course is built slightly smaller than the one below it, until the walls meet at the center, forming a cone-shaped dome.

A thick layer of clay, like plaster, is spread over the bricks. This seals them, making the walls and roof weatherproof.

While the clay is drying, V-shaped patterns are carved on the dome's surface. Besides being decorative these patterns also perform several useful functions. They act as footholds for climbing, and also provide a type of gutter system for rainwater, which otherwise could cause the dome to crack and erode over a period of time.

The Practical Dome

Nomads are people with no fixed home. Often they live in the world's most remote and inhospitable places, gathering food and shepherding their livestock with none of the modern conveniences that make our lives easier.

Because these tribes from the African and Asian continents shift their place of abode once or twice a year, the shelters they live in must be portable, easy to assemble, and strong enough to withstand a harsh climate and the rigors of travel. The tent fulfills all these needs, and dome-shaped tents are by far the oldest and most popular style.

Dome tents are an ideal shelter for dry, hot climates where daytime temperatures vary greatly from those at night. The dome tent, because of its curved surface, absorbs less heat during the day than a tent with a flat roof. Because of the tent's thick cover, it also cools down gradually at night, which means that changes between day and night temperatures are not so extreme and uncomfortable for the occupants.

A minimum amount of material is used to construct a dome tent, and yet these shelters can enclose a large area with few internal obstructions, such as the posts or pillars that might otherwise support a tent roof.

A rounded surface is also stronger than a flat one, and when timber poles are bent in a curve they create a surprisingly tough structure capable of supporting its own weight and that of the tent cover.

The Yurt

The Central Asian yurt is an elaborate tent that can be put together in less than an hour and is easily transported on the backs of two camels. The yurt has a self-supporting frame, circular walls, a domed roof, and a wood crown.

The walls of a yurt are made of split willow poles lashed together with rawhide or other natural materials. The modern yurt, however, may be built with metal rivets and screws.

The *khana*, or wall section, is made like a garden trellis. Several khanas are stretched into a circular ground plan, then are overlapped and bound to each other and to a door frame. Because of the khana's accordionlike construction, it is easily folded and stored for travel.

A *tension band* makes the yurt walls rigid and strong. It encircles the khana like a belt and is fixed to the door frame. Three poles are used to center a wood *crown*, which gives the yurt roof its dome shape. The crown is an important part of the yurt structure because it pushes the roof poles outward, which gives the frame extra strength. Once the crown is in place, the rest of the roof poles may be attached. The other purpose of the crown is to provide a central opening to let fresh air and light into the yurt.

Felt is used for the outer covering of the yurt. This fabric is not woven but made by damping, beating, and rolling wool into wide sheets. As many as eight layers of felt may be used to cover a yurt in winter. Throughout the year this simple covering is often decorated with woven reed mats and colorful trimmings.

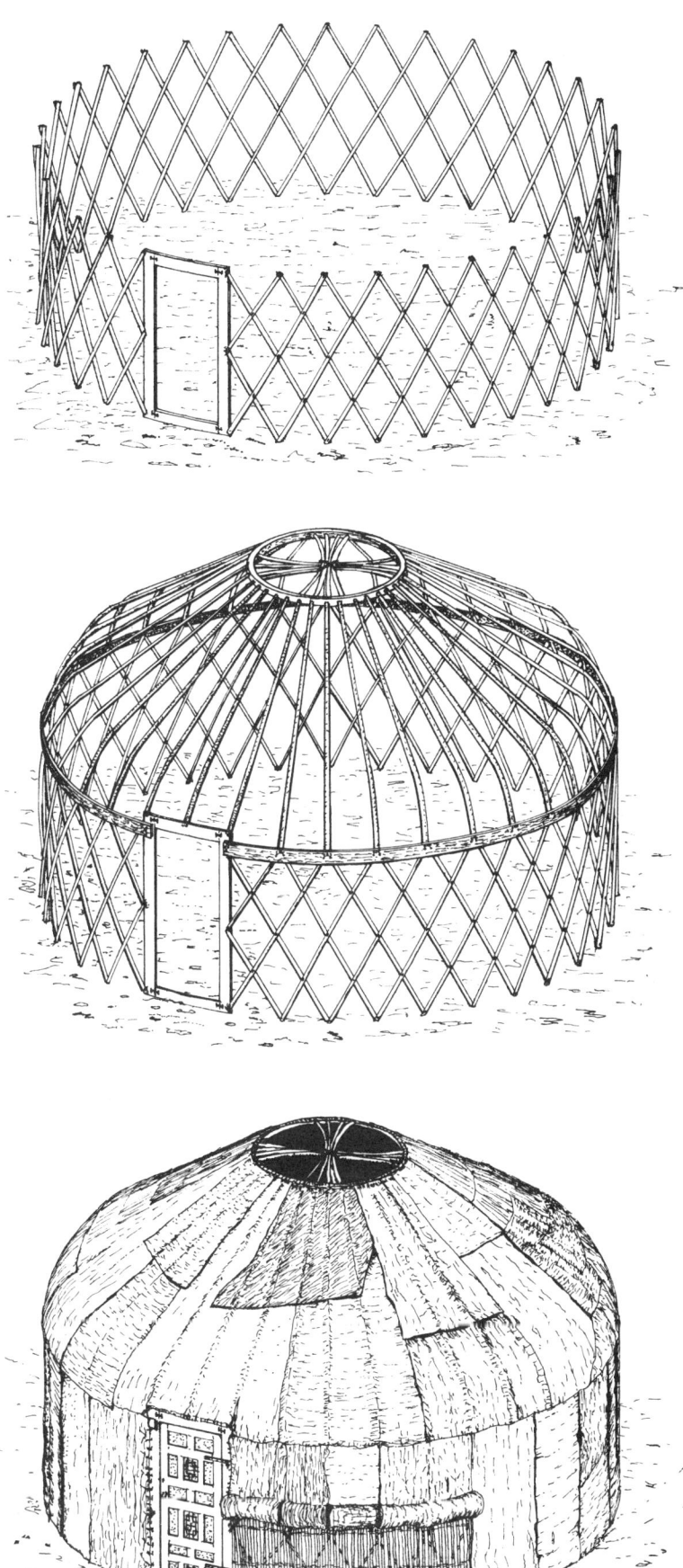

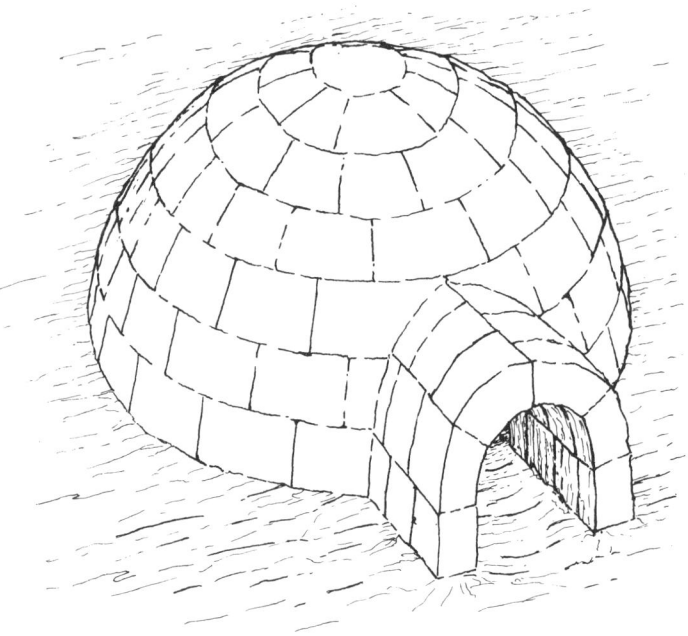

The Igloo

While domes are more frequently associated with hot climates, they can also be found in some of the world's coldest places. The Eskimos of North America and Greenland live in snow domes, known as igloos, for a large part of the year. The igloo doesn't have a frame like the nomad tent. It doesn't need one, because its walls are self-supporting in much the same way as that of the African mud huts.

To build an igloo the Eskimo family marks out a circular space about 3.5–4.5m (10–15ft) across. Traditionally, the man carves snow blocks from the center of the circle, which are then laid around the circle's edge to form the igloo's walls and roof. One opening is left at the top of the igloo and one at ground level. A piece of clear ice is set into the roof opening to provide a skylight or window. The gaps between the rows of blocks are filled with loose snow.

At this point the Eskimo woman takes over. She enters the igloo, lights an oil lamp, and starts a small fire. Then she seals the igloo. She builds up the fire and waits for the igloo's walls to begin to melt. As soon as the walls are moist she reopens the igloo to let the cold air rush inside and freeze it solid. The snow dome is so strong that nothing less than the warm temperatures of spring can destroy it.

To make the igloo more comfortable, seal skins and caribou hides are hung around the walls in such a way as to leave a small space of cold air between the coverings and the wall itself. This space serves to insulate the igloo just as double-glazed or storm windows insulate a conventional house. This system is surprisingly efficient. Igloos can be heated to 15°C (59°F).

II Understanding the Meaning and the Structure

The dome didn't originate from a single source. It wasn't the idea of one person or particular group of people. When domes were first built, people didn't travel across continents as they do now, so the dome shape did not spread through the work of traveling craftsmen or by word of mouth.

Domes appeared in different countries throughout the world. In remote places, where other natural materials were scarce, they were built of clay. In the Middle East domes were first made of wood covered by sheets of metal, while in Greece and Rome domes were built of stone, brick, and concrete.

The shape of domes also varied. Sometimes a dome was rounded like a half circle and known as *hemispheric;* sometimes the peak of its roof was flattened, or sometimes pointed in the shape of an onion. The one thing that all domes had in common, however, was a circular base or ground plan.

The Circle

Philosophers have called the circle the most perfect form. It is. It is a line without beginning and without end—a shape that has had great significance since the earliest of civilizations.

From the beginning of mankind the circle has represented the relationship between life and death. The Romans saw the universe as a perfect circle. The Egyptians worshiped another circle—the sun. Therefore, it was only natural and logical that this shape, with its special meaning, should be used in life (as in the primitive dwellings illustrated in the previous chapter) and also in death (in the design of sacred tombs and monuments).

The Circular Tomb

The circular stone tomb was built as early as 5000 B.C. in countries bordering the Mediterranean Sea. It was built in hollows carved out of the hillsides and, apart from its stone-walled entranceway, known as the *dromos*, it was constructed completely underground.

The *tholos* was a sacred tomb, a hero's shrine, or a monument to a noble family. It was built of hand-cut stone that was so carefully shaped it didn't need mortar to support its beehive-dome shape.

The walls of the dromos (1) were built of heavy sandstone blocks. They acted like retaining walls to support earth piled immediately behind them. The dromos led to a door opening (2) decorated with carved, green-colored stone columns. Finally, a triangular opening (3) was built into the tholos's walls to reduce the weight supported by the door.

The smooth stone walls were sometimes decorated with ornaments, such as bronze rosettes, fixed to the roof. Historians believe that statues, large jars, and altars were placed in the main cell (4) of these tombs. A low doorway (5) led to a rectangular chamber that served as the burial place.

Pictured here is perhaps the most famous tholos: the Treasury of Atreus, or, as it is sometimes known, the Tomb of Agamemnon. It was built in 1325 B.C. on the southeast coast of Greece. Thirty-four courses of stone, capped by a final, carved block, created a chamber that was 13.4m (44 ft) high and 14.6m (48 ft) across.

Understanding the Structure

The staggered stone pattern used to build the tholos was common in early domes. Stacking bricks or blocks to enclose a space in this way—known as *corbeling*—was reasonably efficient as long as the spaces involved were small and the walls could be supported by heaps of earth around them.

The Romans had big ideas for their cities and states, however, so they devised a new type of structure that they called the arch. The true arch was able to span great distances using less material. It also took less time to build than other types of structures. Many Roman bridges and buildings supported by arches are still standing and in use today.

The Arch

The silhouette of any dome is the same shape as an arch and this is no coincidence. The engineering principle of both is exactly the same. Both are *compression* structures, which means that they are very strong when their materials are pressed together under the force of weight.

The arch, as seen here, is built of *voussoirs*, which are wedge-shaped bricks. A larger brick, called a *keystone*, is placed at the center of the arch. It is the last brick to be added and acts like a "key" to lock, or hold, the other voussoirs in place. If the arch is supported at its ends by *abutments* or *buttresses* built against them

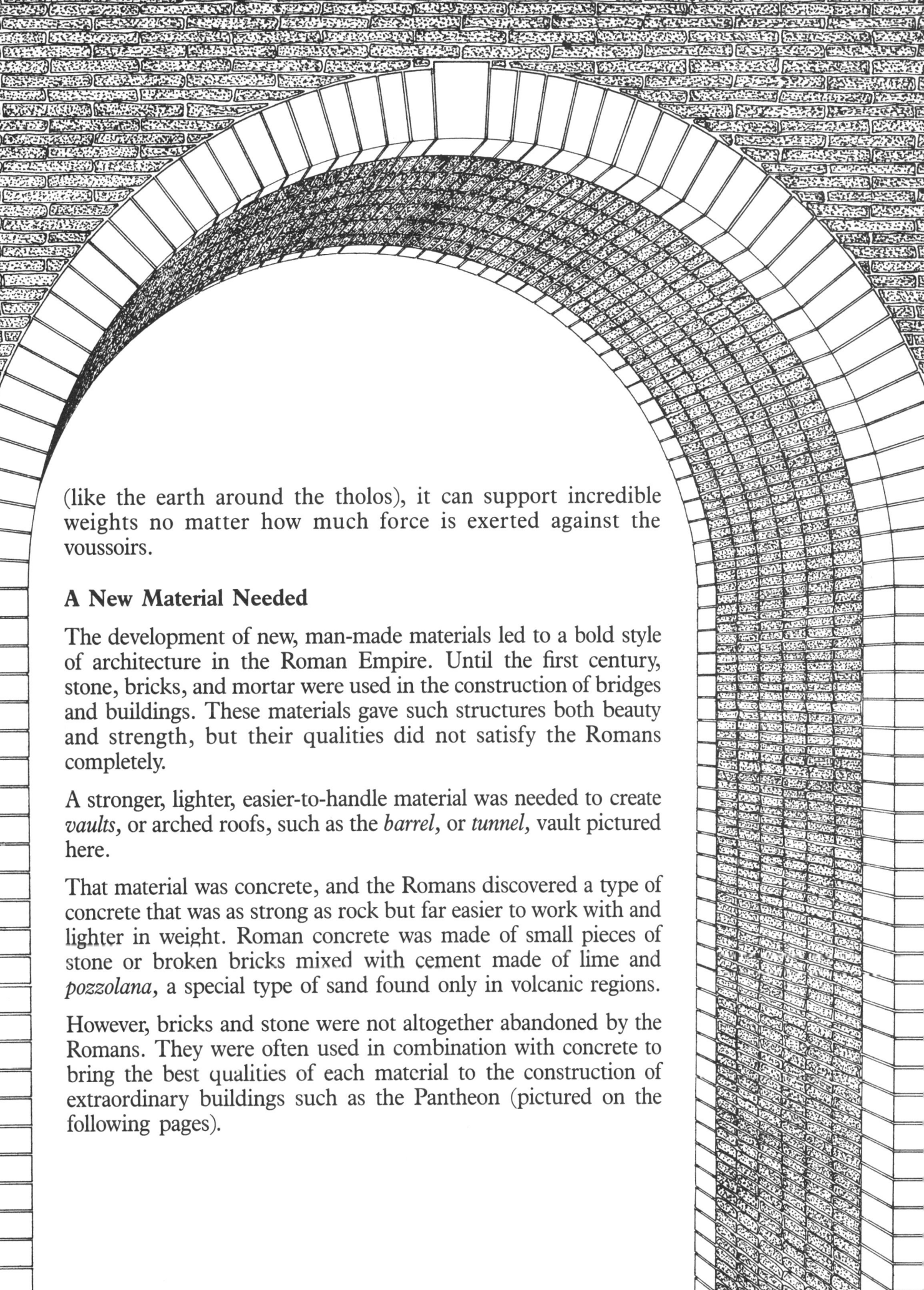

(like the earth around the tholos), it can support incredible weights no matter how much force is exerted against the voussoirs.

A New Material Needed

The development of new, man-made materials led to a bold style of architecture in the Roman Empire. Until the first century, stone, bricks, and mortar were used in the construction of bridges and buildings. These materials gave such structures both beauty and strength, but their qualities did not satisfy the Romans completely.

A stronger, lighter, easier-to-handle material was needed to create *vaults,* or arched roofs, such as the *barrel,* or *tunnel,* vault pictured here.

That material was concrete, and the Romans discovered a type of concrete that was as strong as rock but far easier to work with and lighter in weight. Roman concrete was made of small pieces of stone or broken bricks mixed with cement made of lime and *pozzolana,* a special type of sand found only in volcanic regions.

However, bricks and stone were not altogether abandoned by the Romans. They were often used in combination with concrete to bring the best qualities of each material to the construction of extraordinary buildings such as the Pantheon (pictured on the following pages).

The Pantheon

The Pantheon is one of Ancient Rome's best-preserved buildings. The design is so good it is little wonder it has survived the ages. The Pantheon was first a temple, commissioned by Emperor Hadrian in the year A.D. 124. In A.D. 609 it was consecrated as a church and renamed Sancta Maria ad Martyres. Today it is a reminder of the Roman genius for building, which has had a major influence on architecture throughout the world.

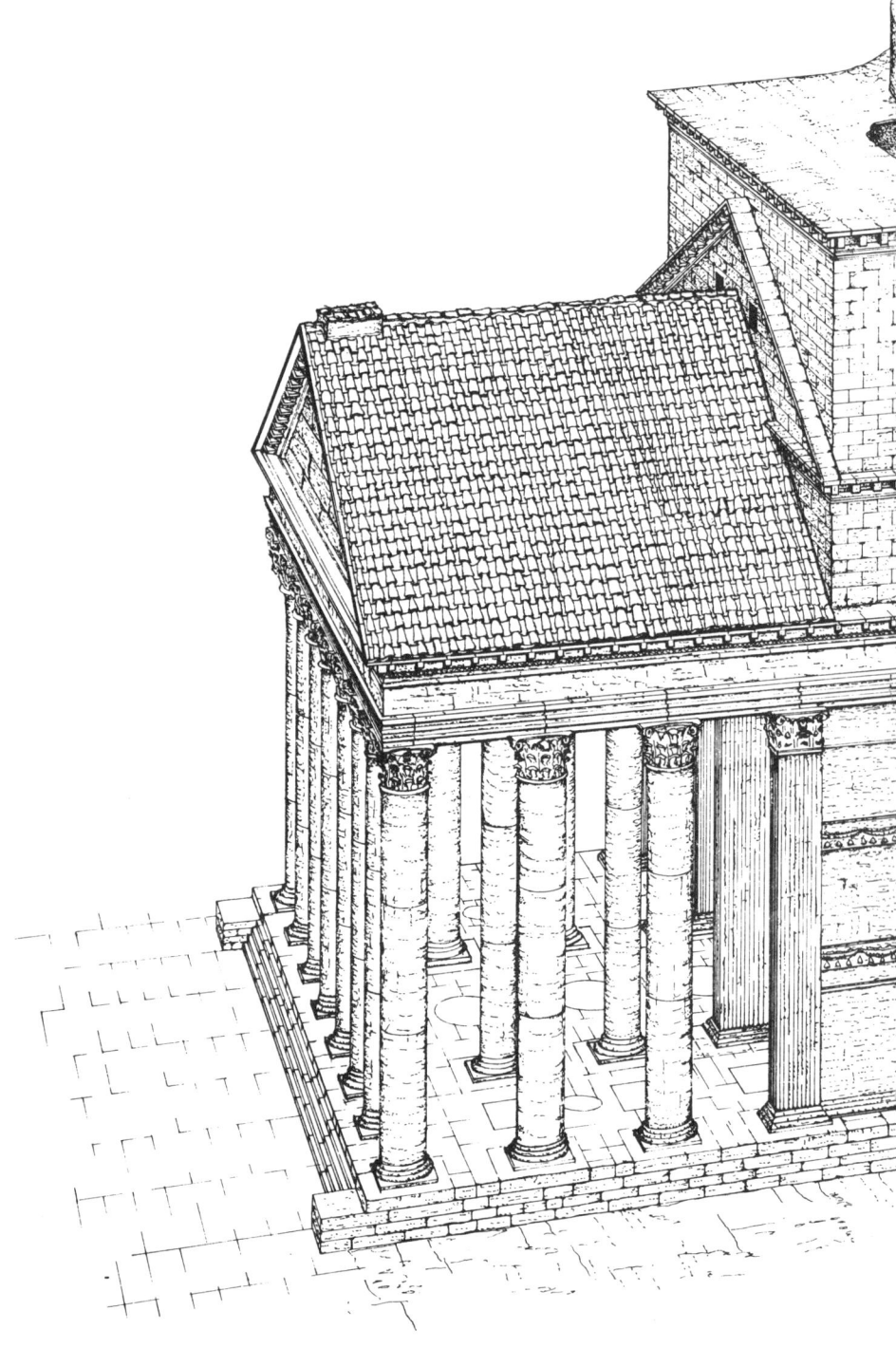

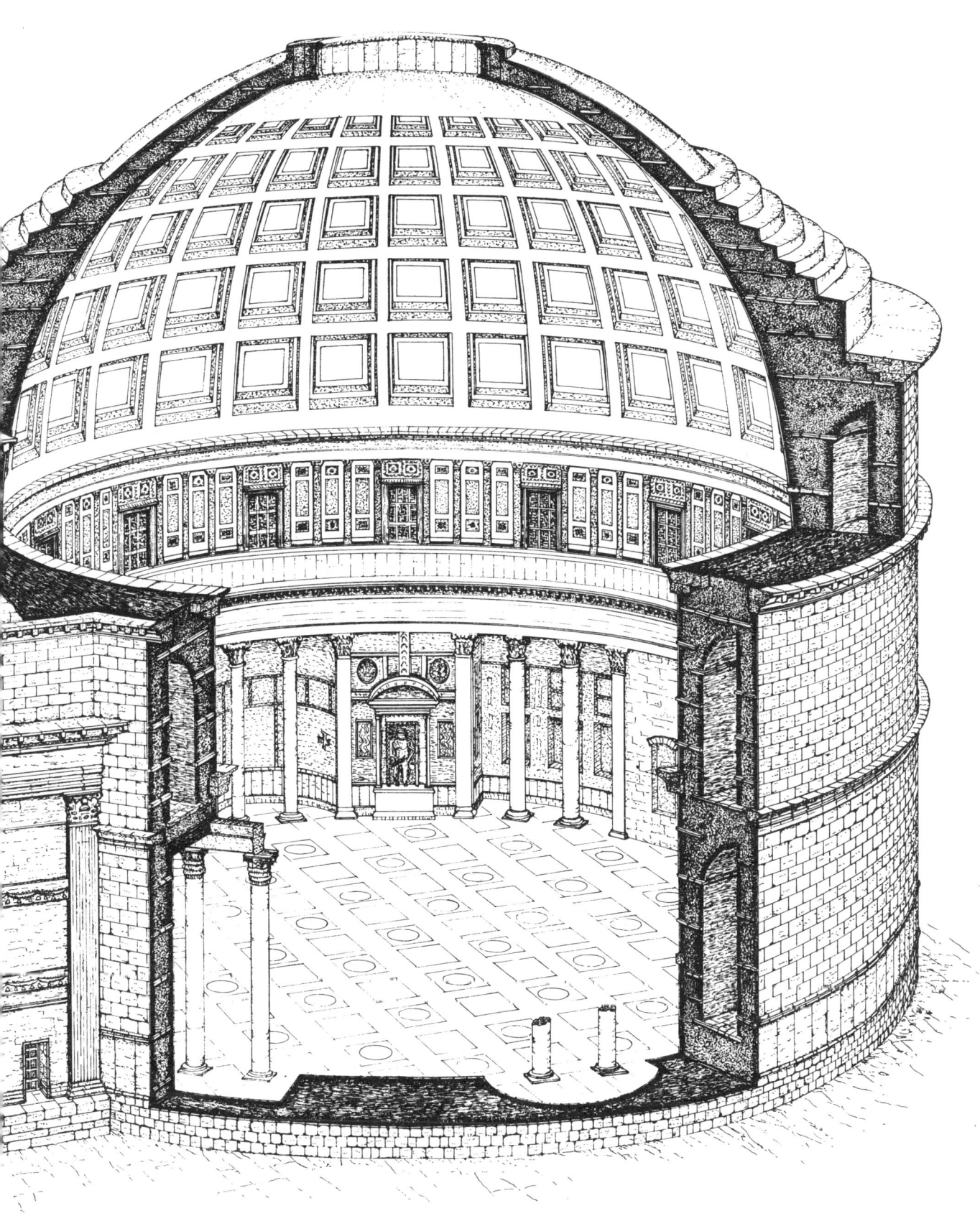

The Pantheon is practically a blueprint for dome building. Many of the engineering ideas used in its superior design were revolutionary for that time, but worked so well that they've been used as the basis for dome building ever since.

The Pantheon's roof, spanning more than 43m (142 ft), was the world's largest dome for more than six hundred years. It was not until the nineteenth century that bigger domes were built, and this was a result of the invention and use of new building materials, not of better dome design.

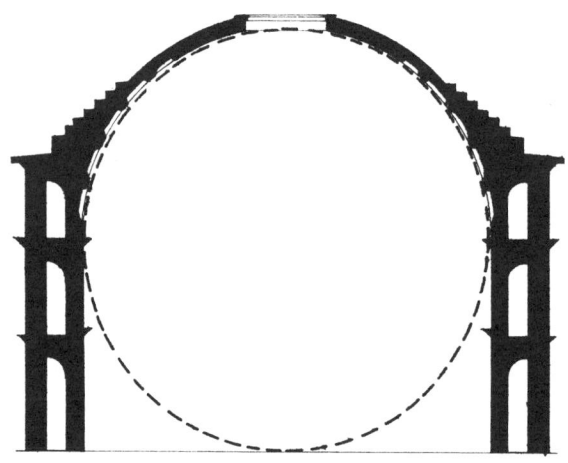

The Design

The circle is the principal feature of the Pantheon's design. The floor plan, the walls, and the roof all have a circular design. The building also has a perfectly circular interior since its height and width are exactly the same: 43.43m (142.5 ft). The circular shape of the building's interior can best be seen in this diagram.

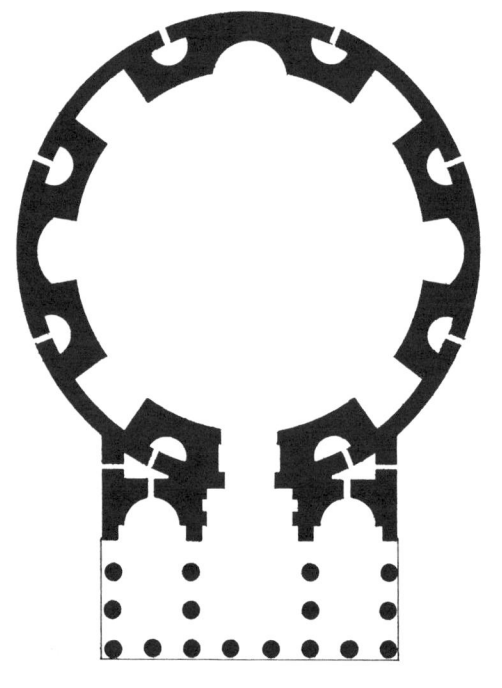

The Foundation and Piers

The Pantheon's foundation is incredibly deep, 4.5m (14.7ft), and wide, 9.8m (32.2 ft). A foundation this size is needed to support the building's eight U-shaped *piers* spaced evenly around the building, the 6.1m (20 ft) thick walls, and the monumental concrete roof. The building's piers and the *niches*, which are the spaces between them, are marked on the diagram.

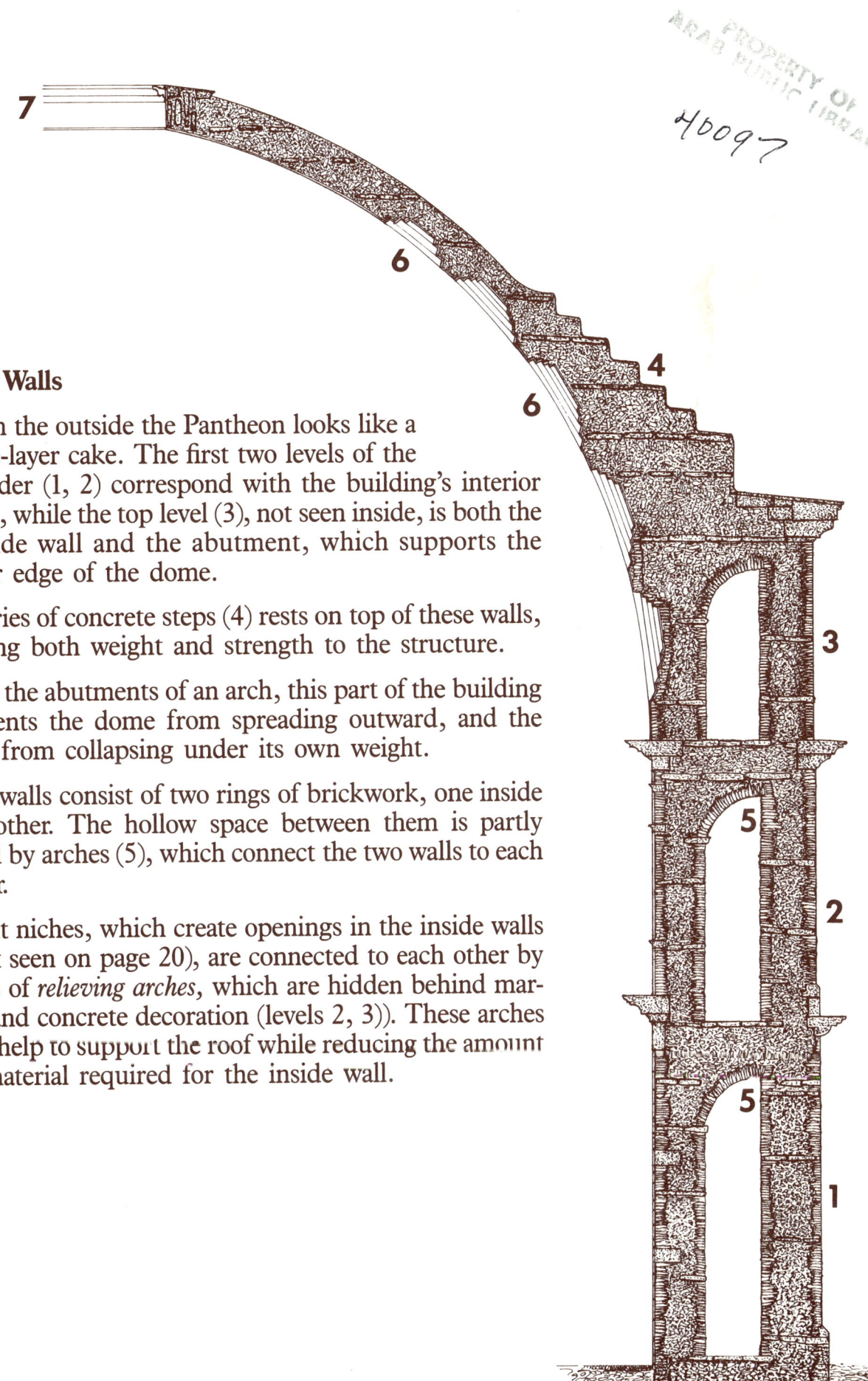

The Walls

From the outside the Pantheon looks like a three-layer cake. The first two levels of the cylinder (1, 2) correspond with the building's interior walls, while the top level (3), not seen inside, is both the outside wall and the abutment, which supports the outer edge of the dome.

A series of concrete steps (4) rests on top of these walls, adding both weight and strength to the structure.

Like the abutments of an arch, this part of the building prevents the dome from spreading outward, and the roof from collapsing under its own weight.

The walls consist of two rings of brickwork, one inside the other. The hollow space between them is partly filled by arches (5), which connect the two walls to each other.

Eight niches, which create openings in the inside walls (best seen on page 20), are connected to each other by rows of *relieving arches*, which are hidden behind marble and concrete decoration (levels 2, 3)). These arches also help to support the roof while reducing the amount of material required for the inside wall.

The Dome

The Pantheon's dome has a complicated wood framework, which has been seen only in part when the building was renovated in 1927. As a result, its design remains something of a mystery, being sandwiched between the roof's two concrete shells.

Lead sheet protects the outside of the dome. The inside is decorated by five rings of box-shaped recesses called *coffers* (6). The gradually thinning design of the roof and the hollowed-out coffers help to reduce the dome's weight so that it can be safely supported by the building's thick walls.

The Oculus

The *oculus* (7), sometimes called the eye of the dome, is the circular opening at the center of the Pantheon's roof. It is 8.23m (27 ft) across its widest part and lined with a ring of brass. The oculus, which also helps to reduce the dome's weight, is the building's only source of natural light.

The structural purpose of the oculus is to act like the keystone of an arch, locking the dome in place and making it one of the greatest compression structures ever designed.

The Roman Contribution

The Romans may be given credit for engineering and architectural design in buildings such as the Pantheon. However, their true genius was in building methods that organized labor efficiently and the invention of superior materials and equipment that made the job of building faster and easier.

While many of these inventions were lost for a time after the fall of the Roman Empire, they were rediscovered eventually and have been used widely in world architecture ever since.

III Circles on Squares

Building a dome on a circular building was undoubtedly an engineering feat, but building a dome on a square or multisided base was quite another matter. It called for a few architectural tricks.

When the Pantheon was built, its roof sat perfectly on its walls—both being circular in shape. Fortunately, temples, tombs, and monuments were traditionally built on a circular plan. The Romans had enough problems building a dome as large as the Pantheon without having the worry of putting it on a square base.

Architectural needs and styles changed, however, and builders were confronted with the problem of fitting round pegs in square holes—or, more precisely, building circles on squares.

A New Era

In A.D. 323 Emperor Constantine moved the Roman capital to a Greek town called Byzantium. The new center was well placed to serve the needs of the state's new religion—Christianity; at the same time it was situated on an important trade route connecting the western part of the Empire with lands to the east.

Byzantium was renamed Constantinople in honor of the emperor, which was the first of many changes to occur during this era in world history. Besides marking the end of the Roman Empire, as it had been known for almost four hundred years, the move also led to the development of a unique style of architecture that was to take its name from the capital where it first appeared in the fifth century—Byzantine architecture.

Domes were the dominant feature of this new style. They appeared on every important building, which always had a square, rectangular, or multisided base. Though no Byzantine dome ever surpassed the Pantheon in size, those built used the new technology that enabled builders successfully to combine circles and squares in dome construction. This technology, together with Roman building methods and traditional designs from the East, resulted in the construction of many beautiful domes.

Hagia Sophia (Divine Wisdom) in Constantinople, a cathedral that later became a mosque, is a masterpiece of the Byzantine style. It was designed by two Greek scholars, Anthemius of Tralles and Isidorus of Miletus, and built by thousands of laborers in less than six years. The design, completed A.D. 538, was simple—a 32.6m (107 ft) dome over a rectangular building, supported by two half domes, four niches, and four massive stone piers.

Courses of clay bricks and mortar, each no more than 50mm (2 in) thick, were bonded together to form the central dome. Forty windows were constructed around the dome's base to reduce its overall weight and provide a source of natural light. The four towers surrounding the building are known as *minarets*. They were added in the fifteenth century when Constantinople was captured by the Ottoman Turks and became a stronghold for the followers of Muhammad and the Islamic faith.

The Pendative

Builders discovered two methods of converting a square space into a round one so that domes could be built on squares, rectangles, or multisided buildings. Both of these are based on the division of the sphere, or perfectly circular ball, and the construction of arches.

The more advanced design is the *pendative*, which was used in the construction of Hagia Sophia and has been used in dome building right up to the present day. The diagram below shows the form the pendative takes.

Basically it is a triangle. To support a dome, four triangles, or pendatives, are linked to each other by arches. Together they create a circular shape on which a dome can be built.

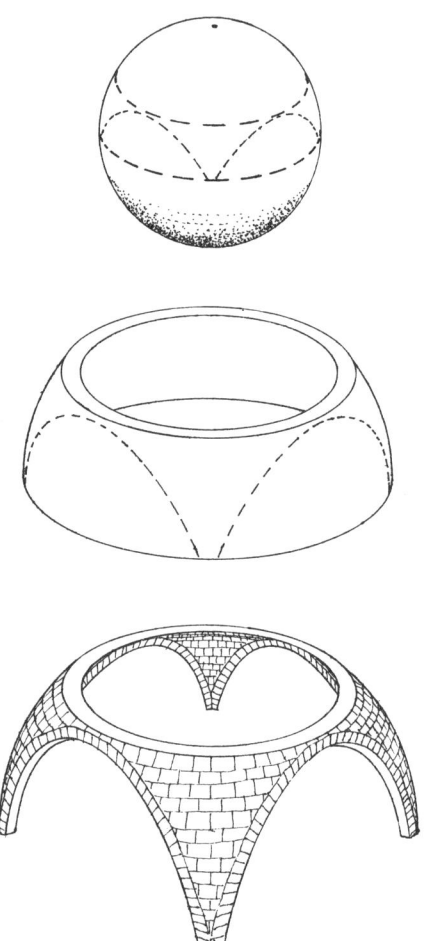

The triangle is the strongest building shape. It cannot be weakened or distorted unless the weight it supports is unevenly placed. When four pendatives are used to support a dome they are incredibly strong. The arches between them distribute the dome's weight evenly over a large area.

The weight is directed through the pillars immediately below the pendatives, and these pillars carry the weight to the foundation of the building.

Pictured on the facing page is the Cathedral of Périgueux, built in 1150 in the Dordogne area of France. At Périgueux, pendatives support five domes, which are placed in the pattern of a cross. This building is a good example of Byzantine architecture; and because its walls are not decorated, it is easy to see how pendatives, arches, and pillars work together to support domes.

The Squinch

The *squinch*, an invention of Western Mediterranean and Central Asian builders, was a simple way of changing the shape of a square or rectangular building to suit the dome's need for a roughly circular base.

The squinch is an arch—or several arches—that bridge the walls of a building, crossing its angles on a diagonal. Squinches, as shown in the diagram below, turn a square into an octagon, an eight-sided shape on which a dome can be built.

Bricks and mortar were most often used to construct squinches, although plaster or fine quality stucco was sometimes used over a timber frame. Besides supporting domes, squinches were also used for decoration. Decorative squinches, call *muquarnas*, were tucked into a building's corners. They were enriched with colorful, honeycomb patterns called *stalactites*.

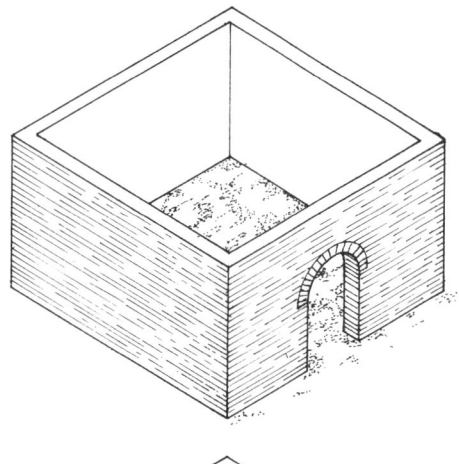

The squinch was first used in Central Asia and North Africa. In the seventh century the teachings of a prophet called Muhammad spread throughout this part of the world and led to the establishment of the Islamic faith. Soon, a style of architecture developed to meet the needs of the new religion.

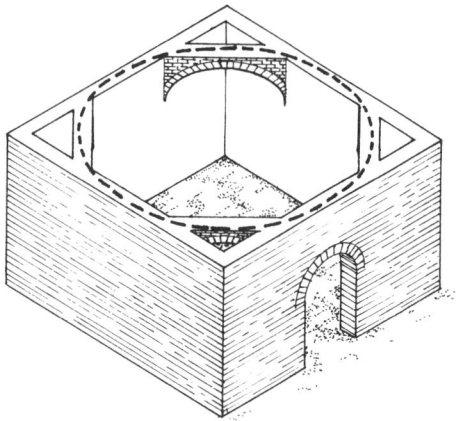

The dome was the main feature of Islamic architecture, just as it had been important to the Byzantine style. The mosque, a place of prayer, was covered by a dome, as were the tombs of the ruling classes. One of these, pictured at right, is the impressive tomb of Tamerlane.

Gur-i-Amir

Tamerlane (Timur), a descendant of the great Genghis Khan, ruled Central Asia in the late fourteenth and early fifteenth centuries. Samarkand (in the U.S.S.R. today), his capital, was filled with extraordinary buildings that were built by architects, craftsmen, and laborers he imported from lands to the east, west, and as far north as Moscow.

Gur-i-Amir, the tomb on the previous page, was built in 1402, in the memory of his favorite grandson, Muhammad Sultan. Tamerlane is also buried there alone with all his male heirs.

The tomb's *gadrooned*, or ribbed, dome resembles a giant melon in shape. It was built on a grand scale: 9m (29 ft) wide, rising to 23m (74 ft) on the inside, and an even grander 33m (108 ft) on the outside.

The bulbous dome rests on a drum and an octagonal base. It is supported by squinches, which are placed where the dome's base meets the tall drum it sits on.

Geometric patterns in various shades of blue are used to decorate the dome, which is covered in glazed matte-finish bricks. The drum, also decorated with tiles, features a repeating pattern in Kufic, or Arabic, letters that reads: "Allah alone is permanent."

When Tamerlane ordered Muhammed ibn Mahmud of Isfahan to design the tomb, the architect built something a bit modest in size. Tamerlane had this first tomb destroyed because he didn't think it was grand enough. It was replaced on the same spot by the tomb that exists today—and took only ten days to build.

HOW TO BUILD A DOME ON A SQUINCH

DOMES MODEL PAGES

Here's how to make a dome on a squinch, like Tamerlane's tomb!

What You Need

Heavyweight art paper or lightweight cardboard, at least 600mm x 500mm (24" x 20")
Medium-weight cardboard, at least 600mm x 500mm (24" x 20")
Tracing paper
Pencil, ruler, scissors, glue

Directions

1. Trace squinch pattern and transfer to medium-weight cardboard. Cut out 4 of these.

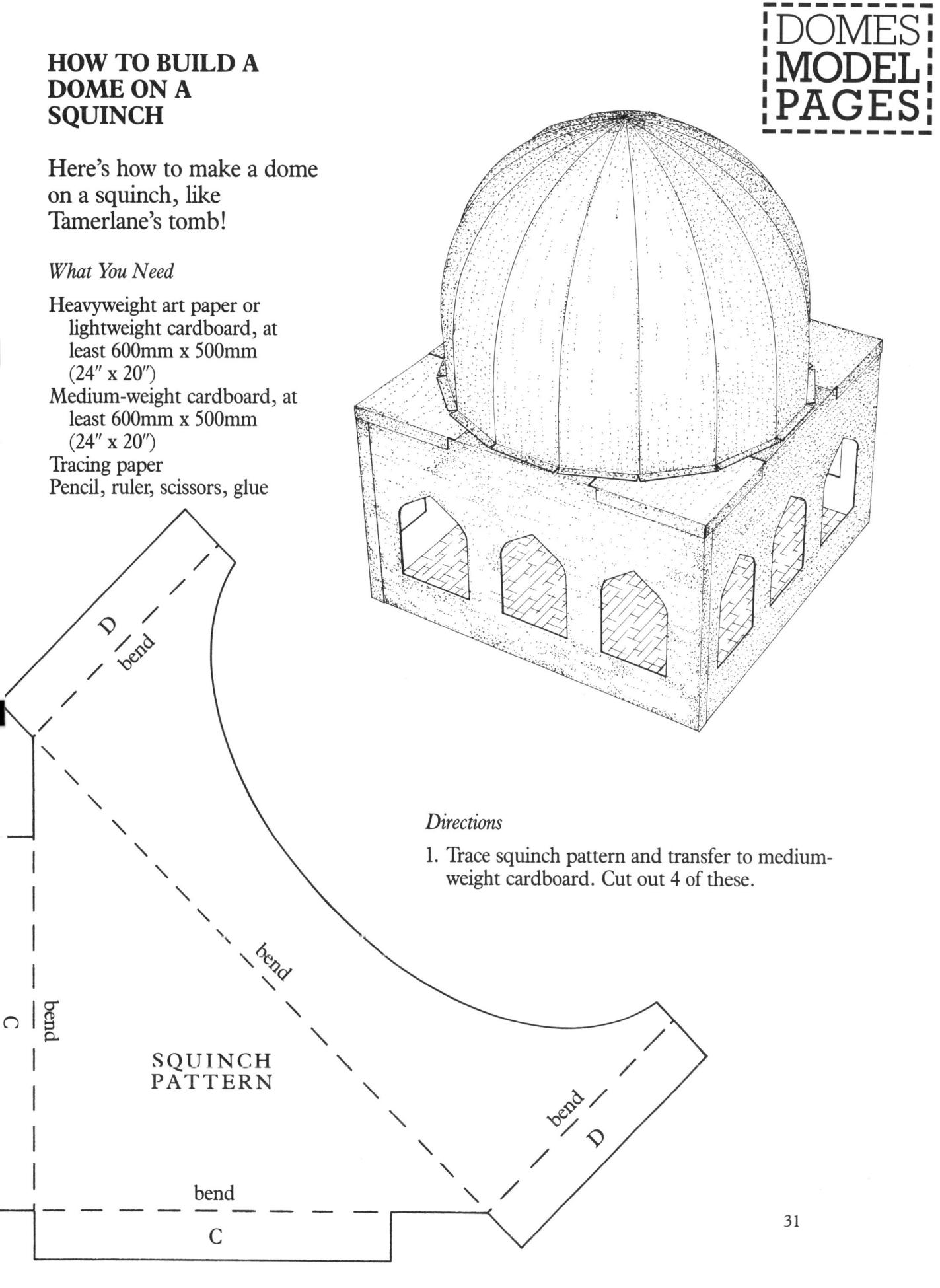

B

bend

WALL PATTERN

WINDOW
(to be cut out
or painted)

2. Trace wall pattern and transfer to medium-weight cardboard. Cut out 4 of these. (You can cut out windows or paint them.)

3. Bend wall patterns along dotted lines marked "A" and glue flaps to join walls as shown. To make cardboard bend easily, draw scissors lightly along dotted fold lines.

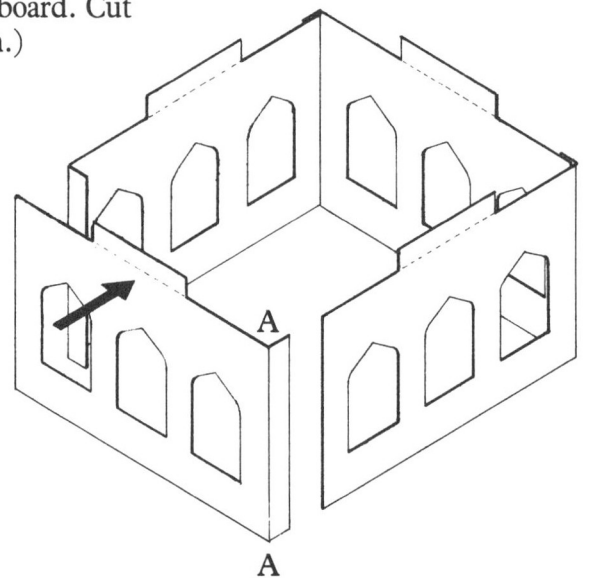

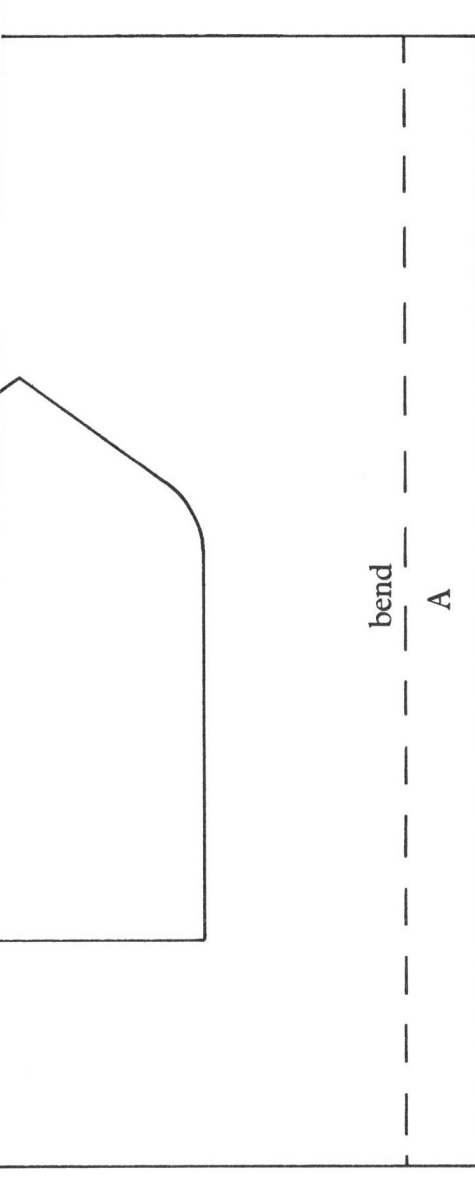

4. To make squinches, bend along all dotted lines, scoring lightly first with scissors. Glue flaps "C" to outside of walls at each corner and flaps "D" to inside of walls as shown.

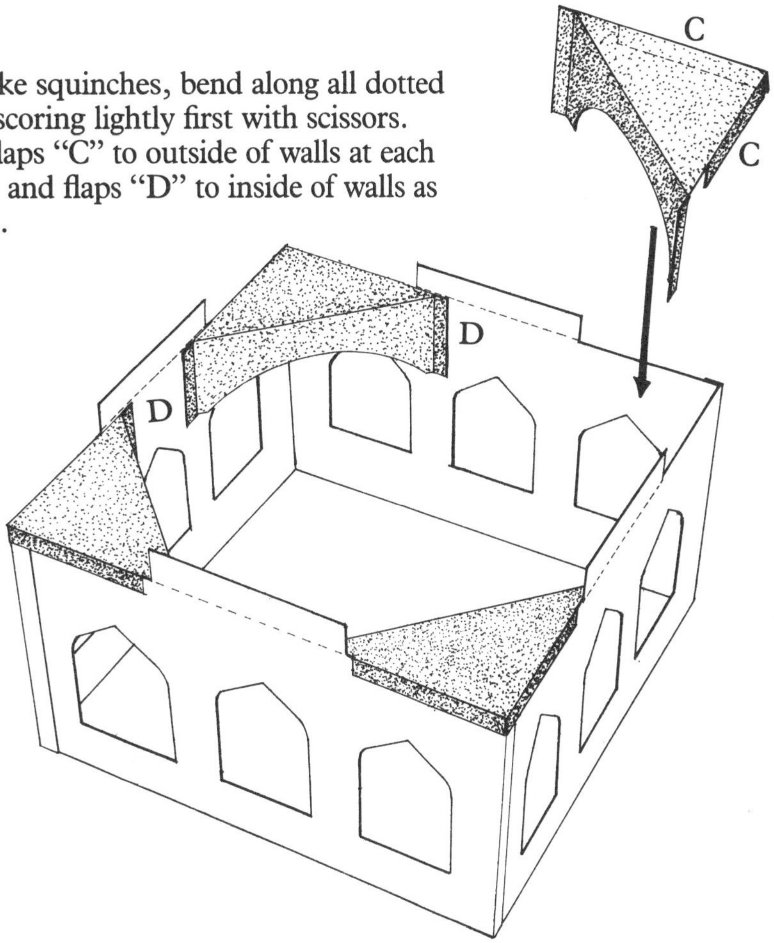

5. Bend flaps "B" on wall pattern and glue to ends of squinches to form base of dome.

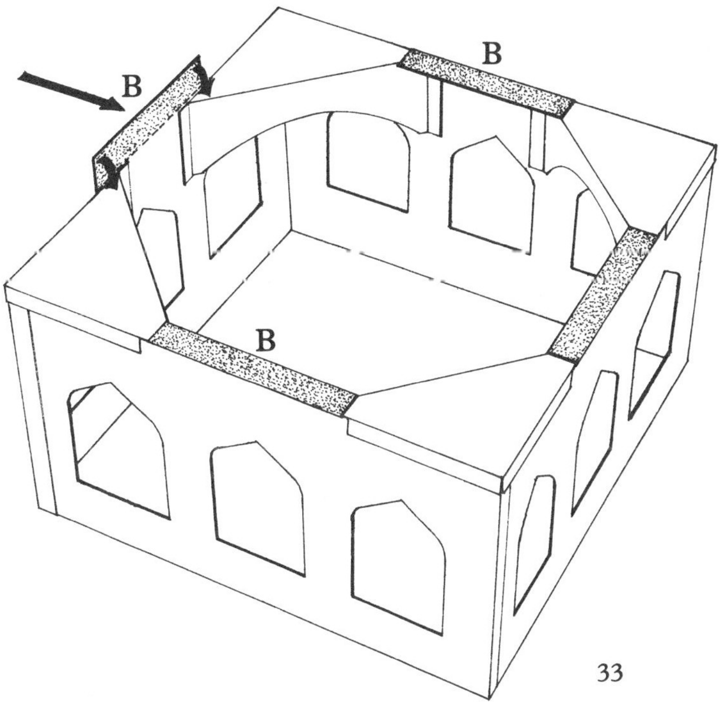

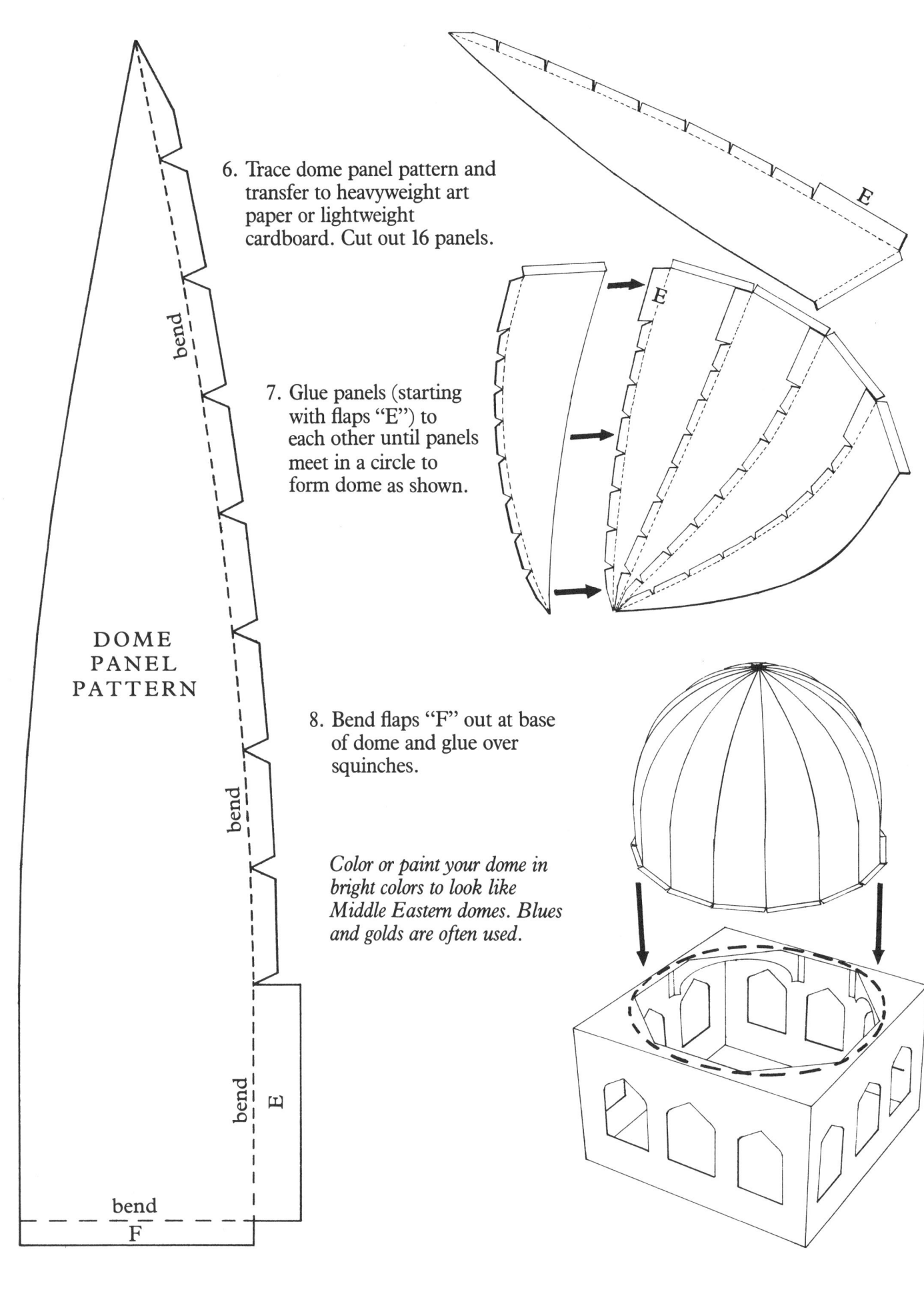

6. Trace dome panel pattern and transfer to heavyweight art paper or lightweight cardboard. Cut out 16 panels.

7. Glue panels (starting with flaps "E") to each other until panels meet in a circle to form dome as shown.

8. Bend flaps "F" out at base of dome and glue over squinches.

Color or paint your dome in bright colors to look like Middle Eastern domes. Blues and golds are often used.

DOME PANEL PATTERN

IV Domes Within Domes

Until the tenth century domes like the Pantheon looked the same inside and out. That's because they were made of a single layer of material that supported itself without the aid of internal columns and beams.

After this time, however, two and three domes were used to cover buildings, and as a result their outside appearance was often very different from their inside appearance. While there are many reasons why domes were built within domes, the most important have to do with the building's appearance, materials, and construction methods.

The Dome—A Symbol

Tamerlane was not unique in his demand for an impressive dome. Most important buildings had domes, so domes came to be associated with greatness. Domed buildings were therefore commissioned by individuals or groups to make themselves, or what they represented, seem important. Many believed that the bigger the dome, the greater they or their organizations would appear.

As a result domes tended to grow bigger, and sometimes more interesting to look at. But while they looked impressive from the outside, many were unattractive inside because they were simply too big.

This problem was sometimes solved by constructing two domes, one inside the other. The inner dome was made to suit the size and shape of the building's interior, while the outer dome could be as different as the builder liked—larger, or in another shape.

Masjid-i-Shah

Double domes were used in countries where bricks and mortar were the main building materials. Rough brickwork on only one surface of a dome could be hidden from view by facing it into the space between the two domes. With the rough brickwork hidden, builders could pay more attention to decorating the visible smooth surfaces of the domes.

The mosque completed in 1638 for Shah Abbas I of Isfahan (above) has two brick domes that are linked to each other by a wooden framework. Located in present-day Iran, it was designed by master architect Abu'l Qasim, who stopped work on the building for two years after the foundations were laid. This delay was to ensure that the building had settled completely and was ready to support the brilliant blue-tiled dome. The inner dome is 21m (69 ft) wide and 35m (115 ft) high. The outer protective dome rises a further 13m (42 ft) to reach a grand height of 48m (157 ft). This cross section shows how different the two domes are.

Double Domes Solve Problems

Filippo Brunelleschi won a competition to design and supervise the building of the cathedral dome in Florence, Italy, in 1420 (see next page). His design was considered a great achievement because it overcame an unusual set of construction problems.

The Problems

Brunelleschi wanted to build a hemispherical dome, thought to be the perfect architectural shape. This was not possible since his task was to build a dome over the existing cathedral (designed two centuries earlier), which had an eight-sided drum (1) on which the dome was to rest.

The dome could not be built over *centering*, a wood framework usually used at that time, since its weight would be too great, and because it was impossible to find trees long enough to span the distance across the 42m (138.6 ft) opening. The dome, therefore, had to be self-supporting while under construction.

The Solutions

Eight major ribs (2) gave the dome its strength and pointed shape. Sixteen minor ribs (3) connected by horizontal ribs (4) strengthened the dome without adding any weight. The pointed shape and ribbed construction produced the least possible amount of sideways force on the dome's base. But to further reinforce this area, heavy wood beams tied with iron rods (5) were added, encircling the dome like a strong belt. The ribbed frame was sandwiched between two domes (6, 7) made of brick and stone, which were laid in a zigzag herringbone pattern. This style of brickwork could be laid without the support of a framework. The stone lantern (8) was completed in 1462. Its heavy weight rested on the ribs, making them rigid and, consequently, stronger.

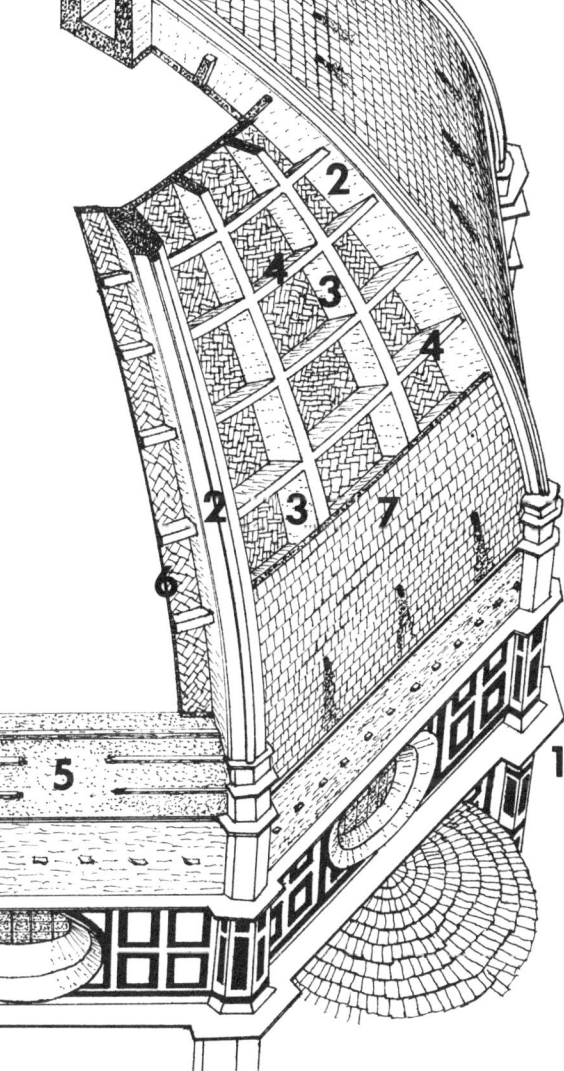

A Triple Dome

St. Paul's Cathedral in London is crowned by a dome that soars 111.5m (366 ft). It was designed by Sir Christopher Wren in 1675 and took about thirty-five years to build. St. Paul's is a dome within a dome within a dome—that is, three domes that span a distance of approximately 34m (112 ft).

The inner dome forms the roof of the cathedral. Like the roof of the cathedral at Périgueux, it is supported by pendatives that rest on eight massive stone piers, through which the dome's weight is carried to the building's foundation. In the center of the painted ceiling of this dome is an oculus, which permits natural light to enter the building through openings in the middle and outer domes.

The middle dome is built of bricks and is only 457mm (18 in) thick. This dome supports an incredibly heavy stone lantern that weighs 850 tons.

The outer dome acts as a protective covering to the other domes. It has a wood framework that is fixed to the middle dome. Its outer covering is lead sheet, a material that has been used since the days of the Pantheon because it is tough, long lasting, and weatherproof.

Like Any Other Dome

St. Paul's weakest point is around its base. To counteract sideways force, Sir Christopher Wren's design called for an iron chain that encircled the dome to prevent it from bursting—an idea borrowed from Brunelleschi's dome in Florence. More than two centuries after the completion of St. Paul's, however, cracks began to appear, indicating that the original chain needed some help. Others were added, primarily in the middle dome, while work was carried out to strengthen the supporting piers.

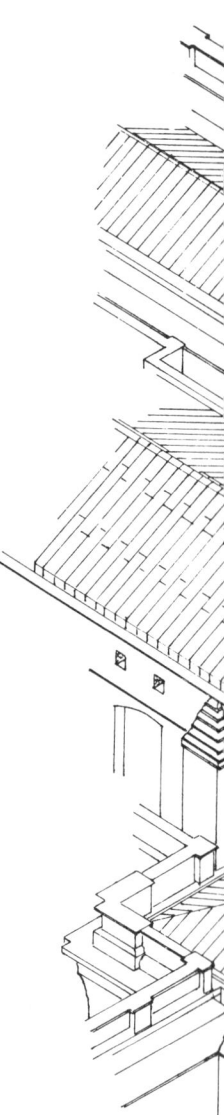

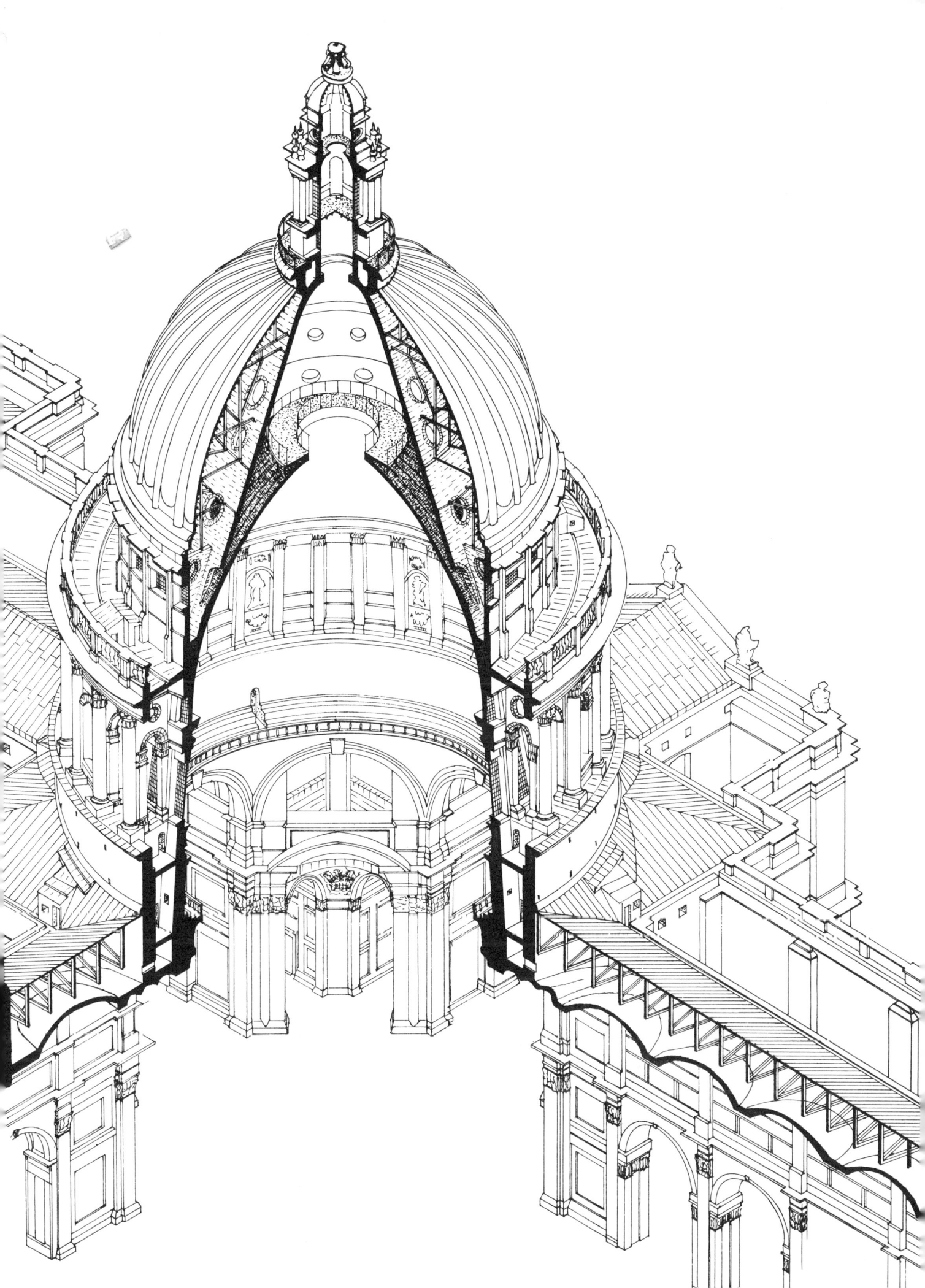

The Hôtel des Invalides

Jules Hardouin Mansart's domed church, Hôtel des Invalides, was completed in Paris in 1691. It, too, had three domes but, unlike St. Paul's, it had one designed for the building's protection and the other two for dramatic effect. The protective outer dome rises to a grand 106.6m (350 ft). It supports a lightweight wooden lantern. The innermost dome, 28m (91 ft) wide, is open at the center to provide a view of the middle dome, which is illuminated by hidden outside windows.

V The Modern Dome

Anything that reduces the amount of natural resources needed by mankind has a future. Any idea that can be used to serve communities in a big or a small way is here to stay. Domes do both—and more.

Unlike many other types of structures, the dome has managed to survive as a building idea for quite a long time. It is true that domes are no longer built as they originally were, but this has to do with the invention of new materials and the improvement of old ones. The basic engineering principles that make domes work as compression structures have not changed at all.

Except in remote parts of the world, domes made of clay, wood, and stone have almost disappeared. They have been replaced by domes of glass, steel, plastics, reinforced concrete, and other man-made materials, materials that are capable of making them bigger, stronger, and more useful than ever before.

Practical Structures

The dome's shape enables it to maintain a steady temperature better than most structures. This has been proved in the felt-covered tents used by nomads. In today's world, this means domes make better use of energy resources like oil for heating.

Domes also use far less material to enclose a space than is required by a square or rectangular building. This often makes domes less expensive to build than other types of buildings that cover the same amount of ground.

Domes can be built quickly and easily. Often they are prefabricated in a factory and are collapsible and easy to transport, which makes them practical and suitable for emergency shelters.

New materials, modern technology, and a suitable shape make domes useful for many purposes, from providing a simple shelter to covering an enormous sports stadium. They are capable of serving a family—or crowds of thousands!

Palazzetto dello Sport

The Palazzetto dello Sport was completed in 1960 for the Olympic games held in Rome that same year. This space-age arena was designed by Pier Luigi Nervi and A. Vitellozzi using concrete, the material that was used in the construction of Rome's Pantheon nearly two thousand years earlier.

Steel, one of the strongest man-made materials, has been used for the dome's frame. The roof, with a central oculus, is made of coffered panels in 19 different sizes out of precast, steel-reinforced concrete. The panels were made in a factory instead of being cast at the building itself. This is a far more efficient way to construct buildings since it saves builders' time and guarantees that the individual panels will be of high quality.

A Clear View

Thirty-six Y-shaped posts support the ends of the 61m (200 ft) dome. These Y posts carry the building's weight—not in a vertical direction but at an angle—to the circular foundation, which extends underground beyond the building we see above ground. That's because these pillars are very much a part of the dome itself. They continue the natural curve of the dome's arch.

The Y-shaped pillars are connected to vertical posts just inside the building to support the roof as well as the seating. Because they are behind the rows of seats, every spectator has a clear view of the field, which he hadn't in square or rectangular buildings of old, where posts were placed within the seating area to support a roof.

The Palazzetto dello Sport was clearly inspired by earlier domes, particularly the Pantheon. However, its practical design, which accommodates up to five thousand people in comfort, is a result of strong and versatile new materials.

Something New and Exciting

An exhibition held in Cologne, Germany, in 1914 brought together new designs by German architects who had organized themselves into a working group called Deutsche Werkbund.

Many of the pavilions designed for this exhibition had merit since they used the materials being developed for industrial purposes at that time in new and interesting ways.

One building in this exhibition, the Glass House, was considered the most exciting because of the new way it used glass and metal in a dome shape (see next page).

The building's design was so different from those before it that it influenced a new architectural style—one that led to the development of the geodesic dome in America in the 1930s.

Glass: A New Use for an Old Material

Glass sheet was first made in Germany in the eleventh century. The processes used in its manufacture have not changed, though modern technology has led to more efficient mass production, better quality, and lower costs.

Glass was used only to a limited extent in architecture up to the late nineteenth century because it was so expensive to make in quantity. By the 1914 exhibition this was no longer the case and, to prove the point, the German glass industry sponsored the construction of the Glass House to show the good qualities of the material and the exciting ways it could be used in architecture.

Bruno Taut designed the Glass House, which, apart from being a display in itself, contained exhibits of other glass products made in Germany at that time. The pavilion was built on a concrete base and, to make the dome appear taller, it was raised higher than the buildings around it. The 16-sided building had walls made of glass bricks, outdoor glass staircases, and a double-domed roof. The outer dome was built of glass panels set in an interlocking framework made of steel ribs. The inner dome was also made of glass and had an oculus through which the outer dome could be seen.

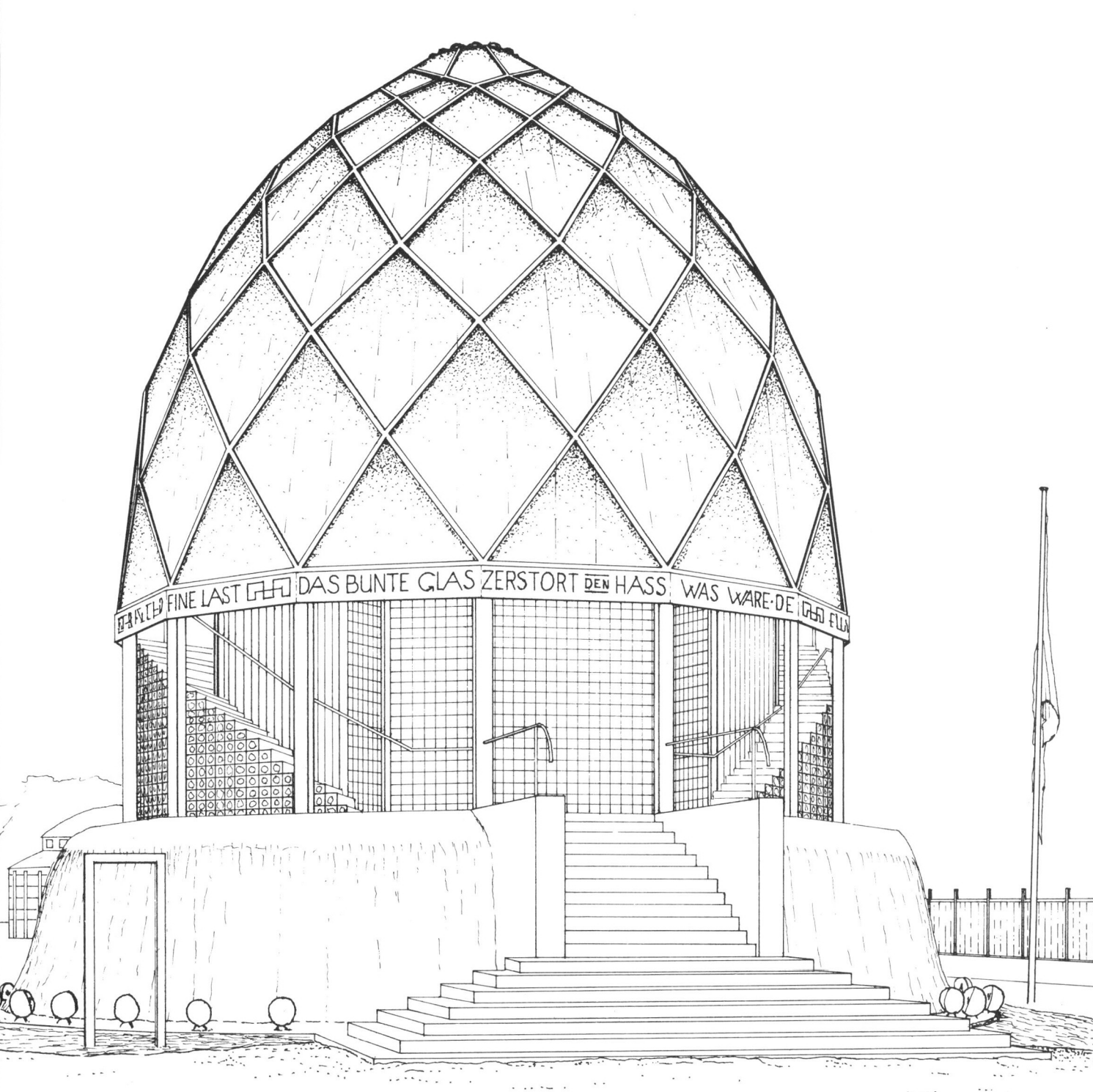

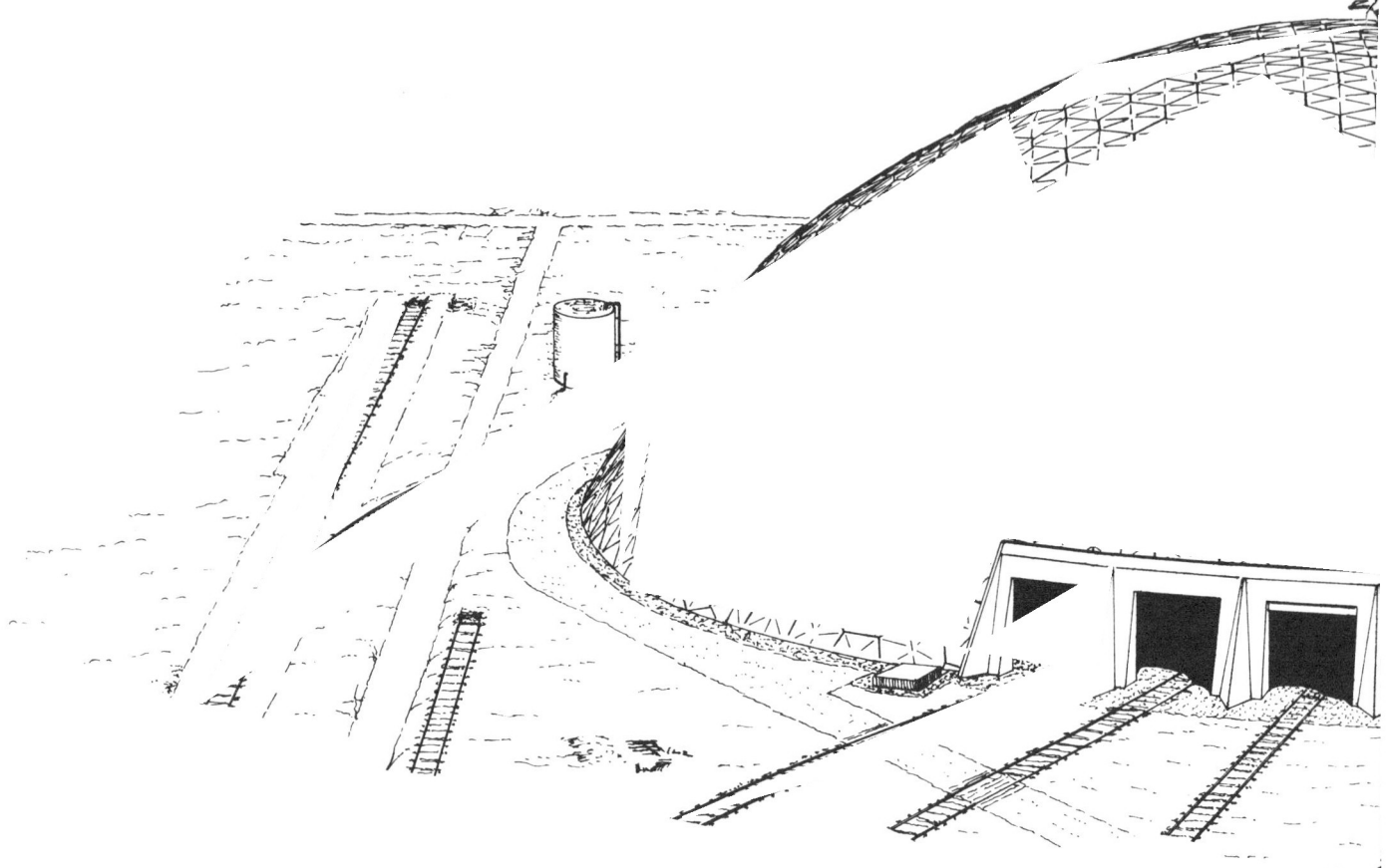

At Last—The Geodesic Dome

Geodesic domes are a modern invention, but their origins go back to early Greek astronomers who divided spheres to make the first planetariums, which showed the movement of the earth, the stars, and other planets.

Geodesic domes are well known because of their recent development and because they received so much publicity as a result of the pioneering work of an American, Buckminster Fuller. Fuller believed that geodesic domes, capable of covering enormous areas, could be used not only to house a family or a factory, but an entire city. He designed a dome that would cover an area of New York's Manhattan Island 3.2 kilometers (2 miles) wide. In theory, this dome could be built in three months with the help of helicopters.

Fuller believed that people should control their environment to create the best possible living conditions for themselves, and that domes would be suitable for this purpose. If air and water pollution continue to increase throughout the world, domes, as Fuller imagined them, could become necessary for man's survival.

Fuller's first experiments with geodesic domes began in 1927. However, it was not until 1945, when his portable dome house—the Dymaxion Dwelling Machine—was exhibited, that he could convince people of the dome's usefulness.

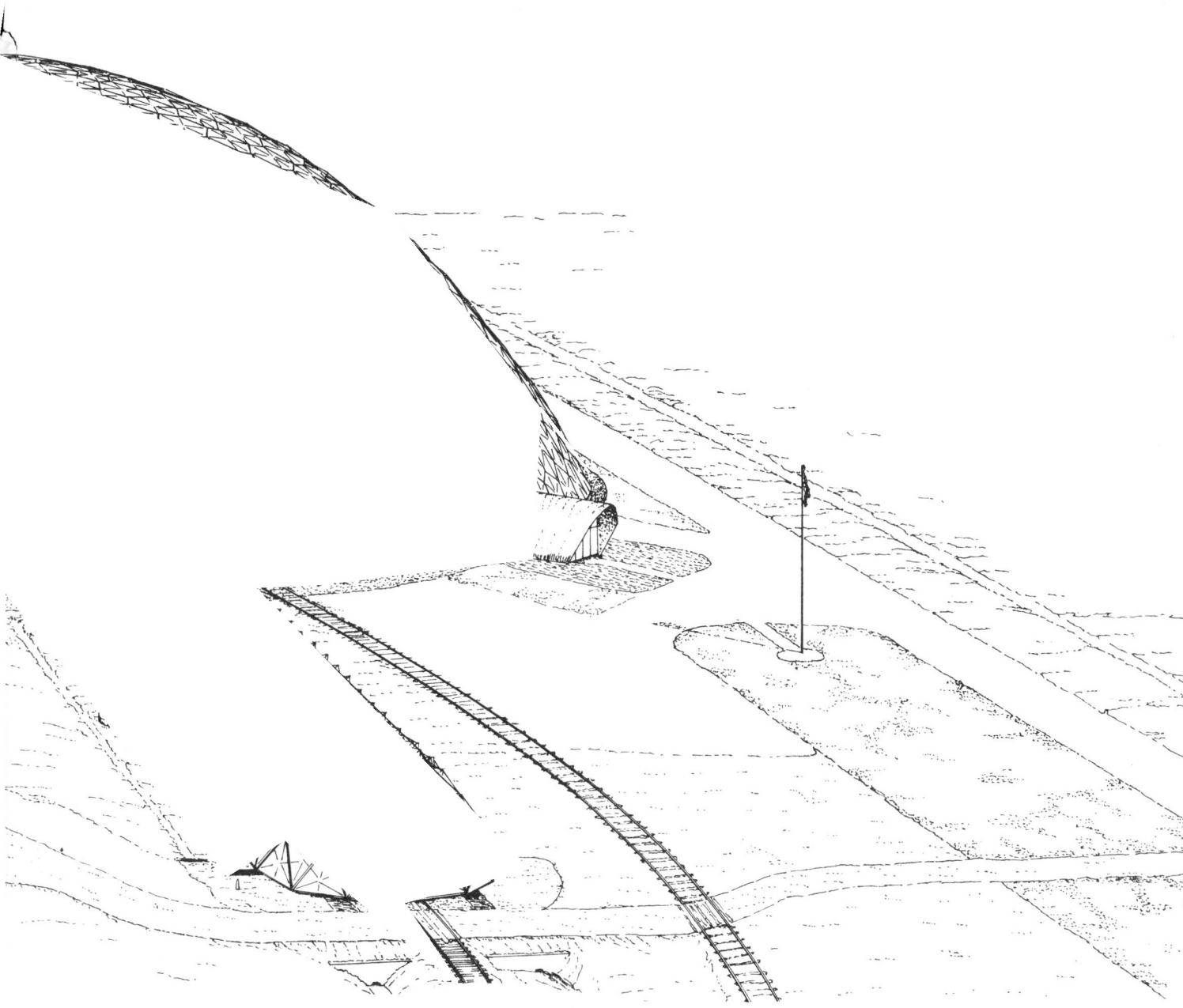

In 1958 he completed the dome pictured here—the Union Tank Car Company building in Baton Rouge, Louisiana. It is as tall as a 10-story skyscraper (35.4m, 116 ft) and wide enough to cover a football field (117m, 384 ft). The steel-frame dome contains an inner dome that is used as the main car-repair unit. A 61m (200 ft) tunnel leading to the building serves as a paint shop. When it was completed, the Tank dome was the biggest of its kind ever built.

How Practical Are They?

The geodesic dome is particularly useful for buildings that are used by many people at one time, such as sports arenas and factories. The main problem with using them as individual houses is that they are difficult to divide into separate rooms.

Because air circulates freely within a dome, occupants enjoy a comfortable climate twenty-four hours a day. However, when walls are added inside a dome, air movement is restricted and it is difficult to control temperatures throughout the house.

Geodesic domes are used primarily because they are less expensive to build than many other types of houses. The geodesic dome also suits the nomadic life-style of many people today, since, like tents, domes can be taken apart and reassembled at another place without much effort.

Geodesics can sometimes use modern technology to create better living conditions on a small scale. A perfect example of this is the Desert House built in Arizona in 1952 by Paolo Soleri and Mark Mills. This house featured a glass dome that moved according to temperature changes inside and outside the building. The dome would open to let in cool air, and close when no more was required. Clearly, domes have come a long way from those built by the earliest civilizations.

How They Really Work

The geodesic dome gets its name from Greek words meaning earth dividing. A geodesic dome is therefore made by dividing a sphere into a series of triangles. A very strong structure can be built by placing triangles side by side. In the geodesic dome, the sphere is divided by as many triangles as are required—the more used, the stronger the structure. All the sides of these triangles, usually made of steel, work together to spread weight and stress evenly throughout the structure.

HOW TO MAKE A GEODESIC (EARTH DIVIDING) DOME

DOMES MODEL PAGES

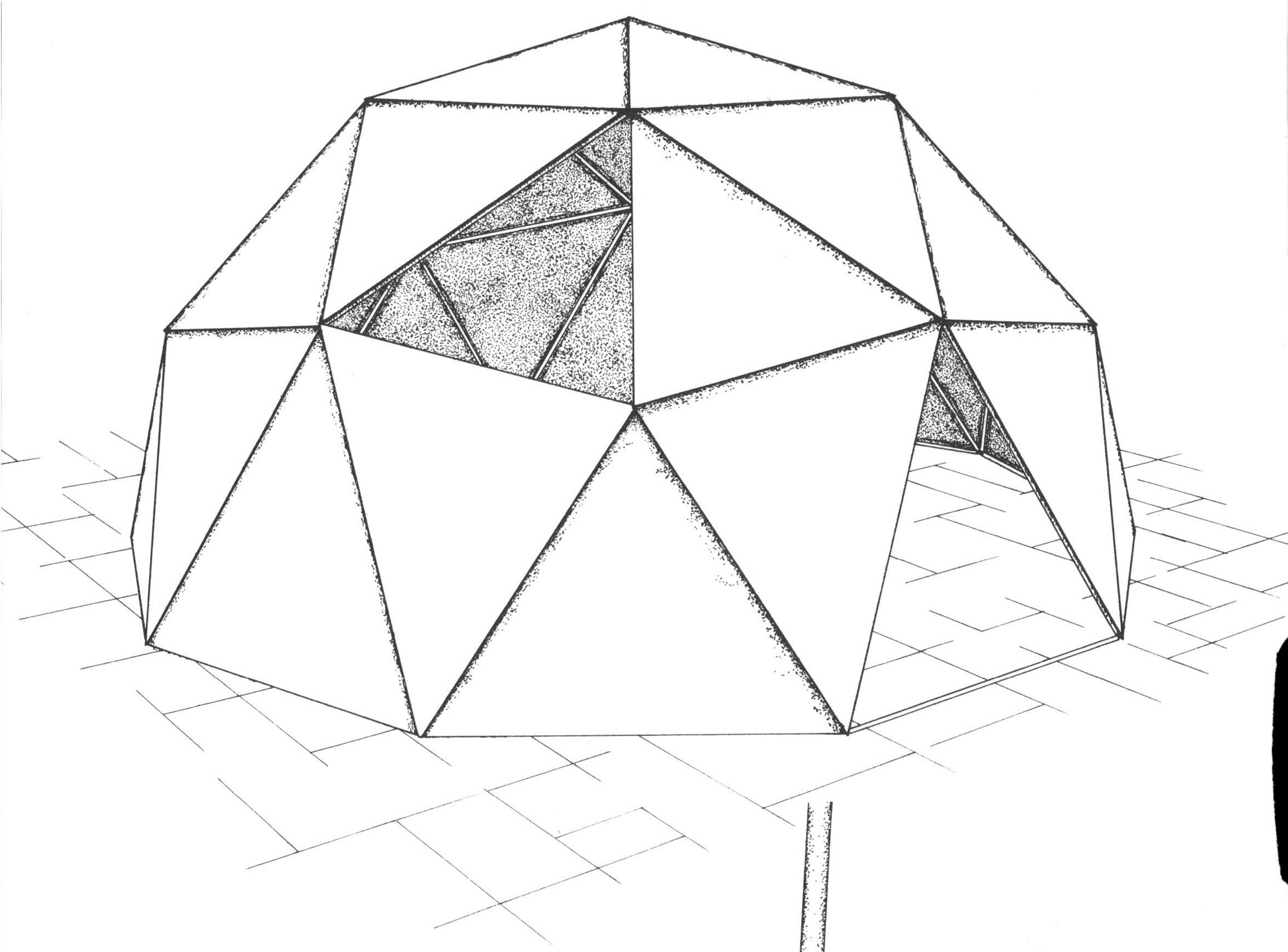

What You Need

33 pipe cleaners, each to be cut into 4 pieces about 40mm (1½") long. In the directions these pipe cleaner pieces will be called PCP.

65 thin paper straws (35 to be cut into LONG 200mm (8") pieces; 30 to be cut into SHORT 180mm (7¼") pieces). Plastic straws may be used but may need to be glued at joints.

Heavyweight paper or lightweight cardboard, at least 4 sheets 600mm x 500mm (24" x 20").

Pencil, ruler, scissors, glue.

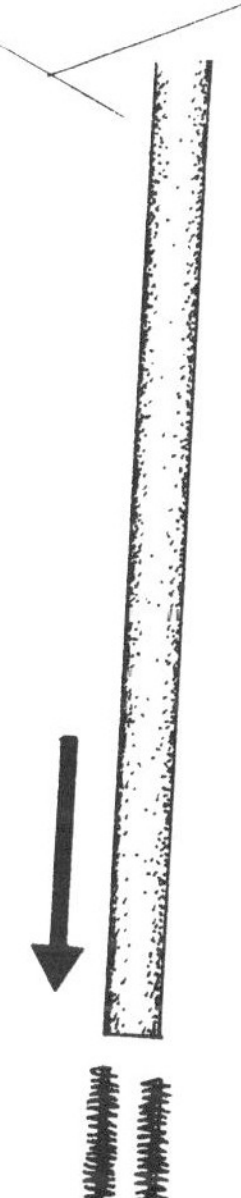

General Instructions

To put triangles together, bend pipe cleaner pieces (PCP) in half. Push 2 together into end of each straw to make a tight-fitting joint.

These joints connect the sides (straws) of the triangles, which are the basic units of the geodesic dome model.

51

Directions

1. Join 10 LONG straws in a circle. Use 3 PCP for each joint as shown below.

2. Connect 1 LONG and 1 SHORT straw to each joint with another PCP as shown. It is important to group straws in pairs around circle: 2 SHORT, 2 LONG, 2 SHORT, etc.

3. To make 10 triangles, join ends of straws with 3 PCP as shown below.

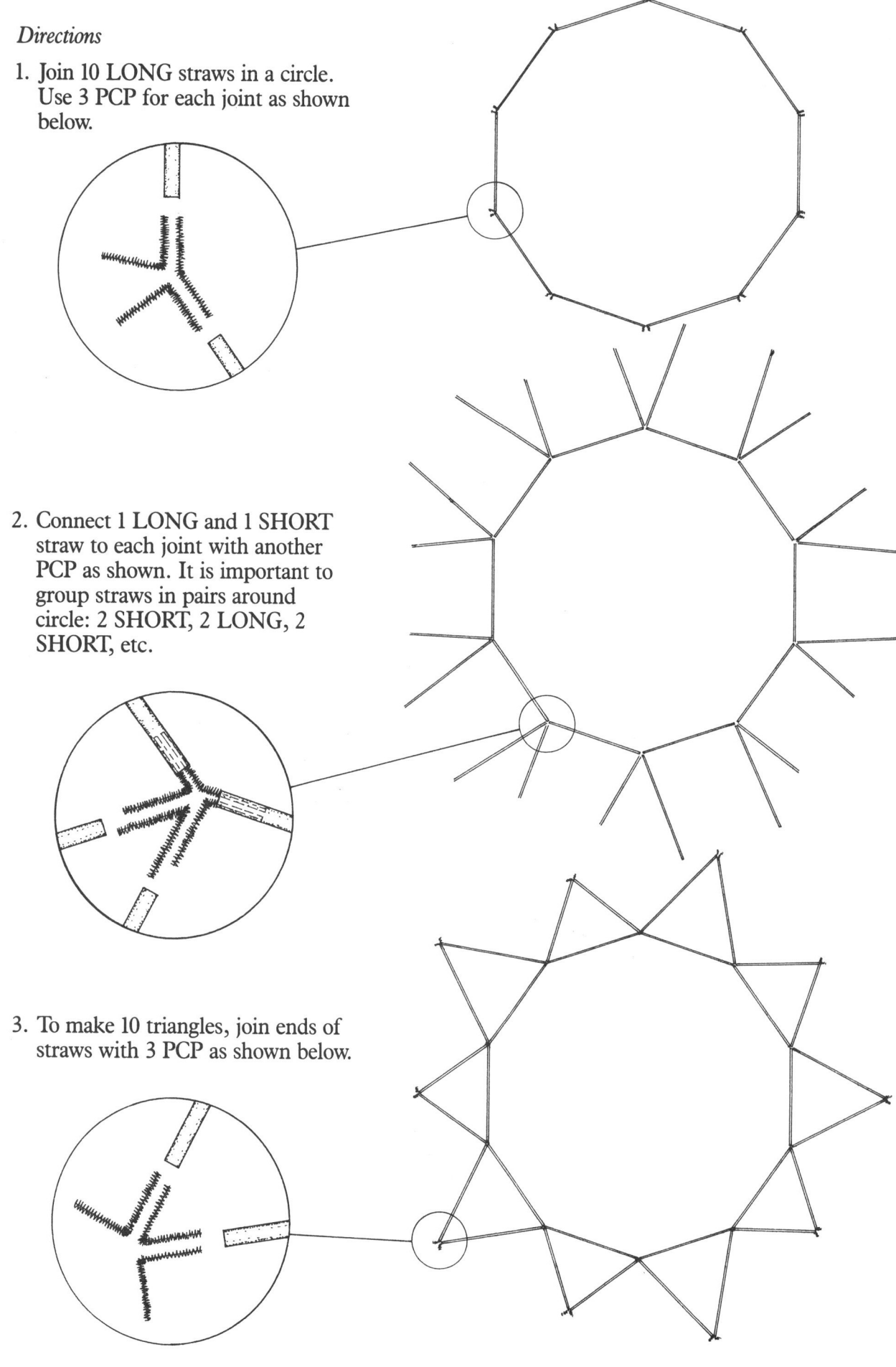

4. Push triangles up and join tops of triangles with 10 SHORT straws, using 2 more PCP.

5. Where 4 SHORT straws meet, add 1 more SHORT straw as shown below. These 5 joints are now complete.

6. Add 2 more LONG straws, using a PCP, to joints that remain. These 5 joints are now complete.

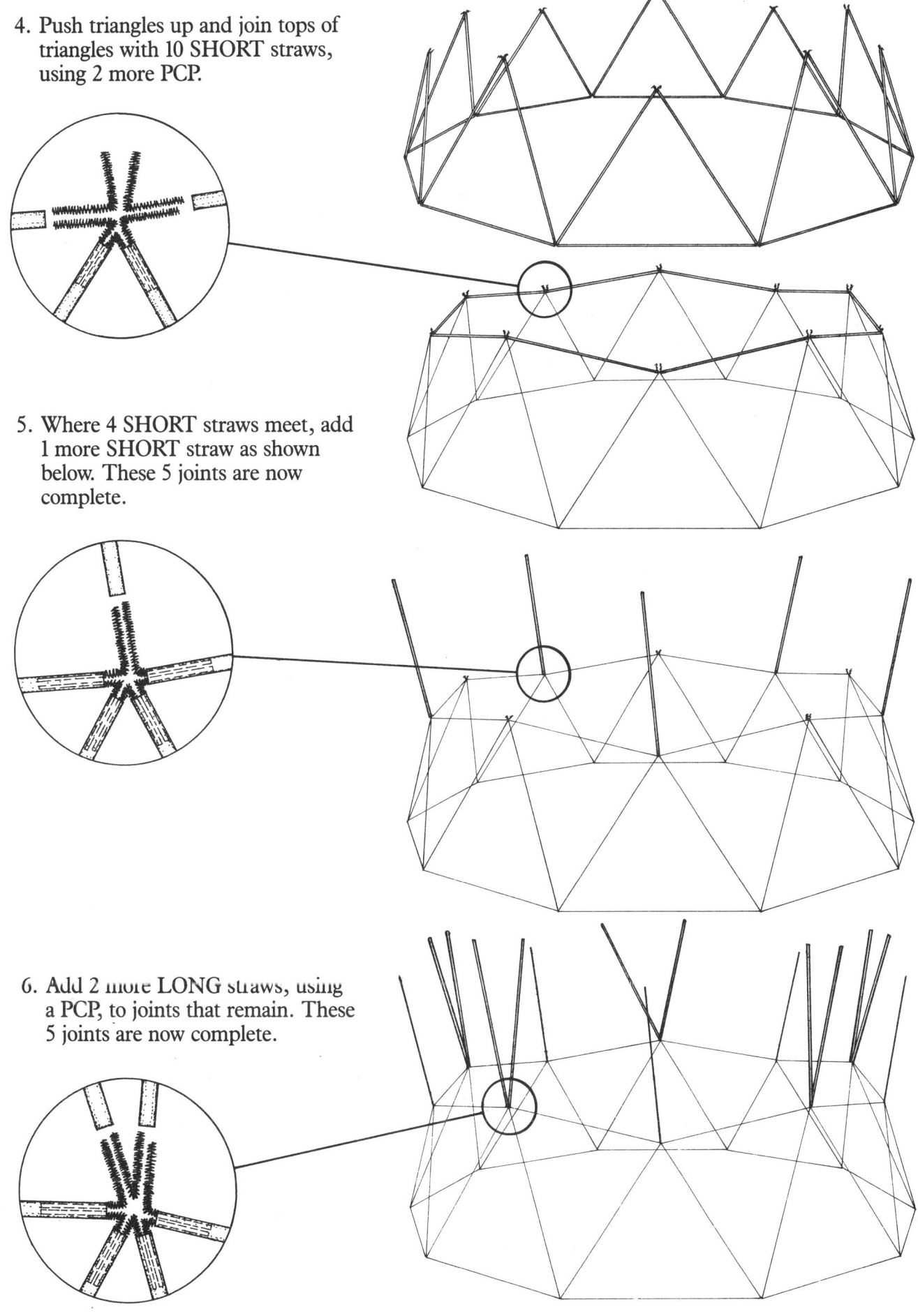

7. Join 3 straws to each other, using 4 PCP, as shown below. (You should be joining 1 SHORT straw between 2 LONG straws.)

8. Use last 5 LONG straws to connect triangles with 2 PCP at each joint.

9. Add last 5 SHORT straws as shown. Join them at center, using 5 PCP, to complete geodesic dome frame.

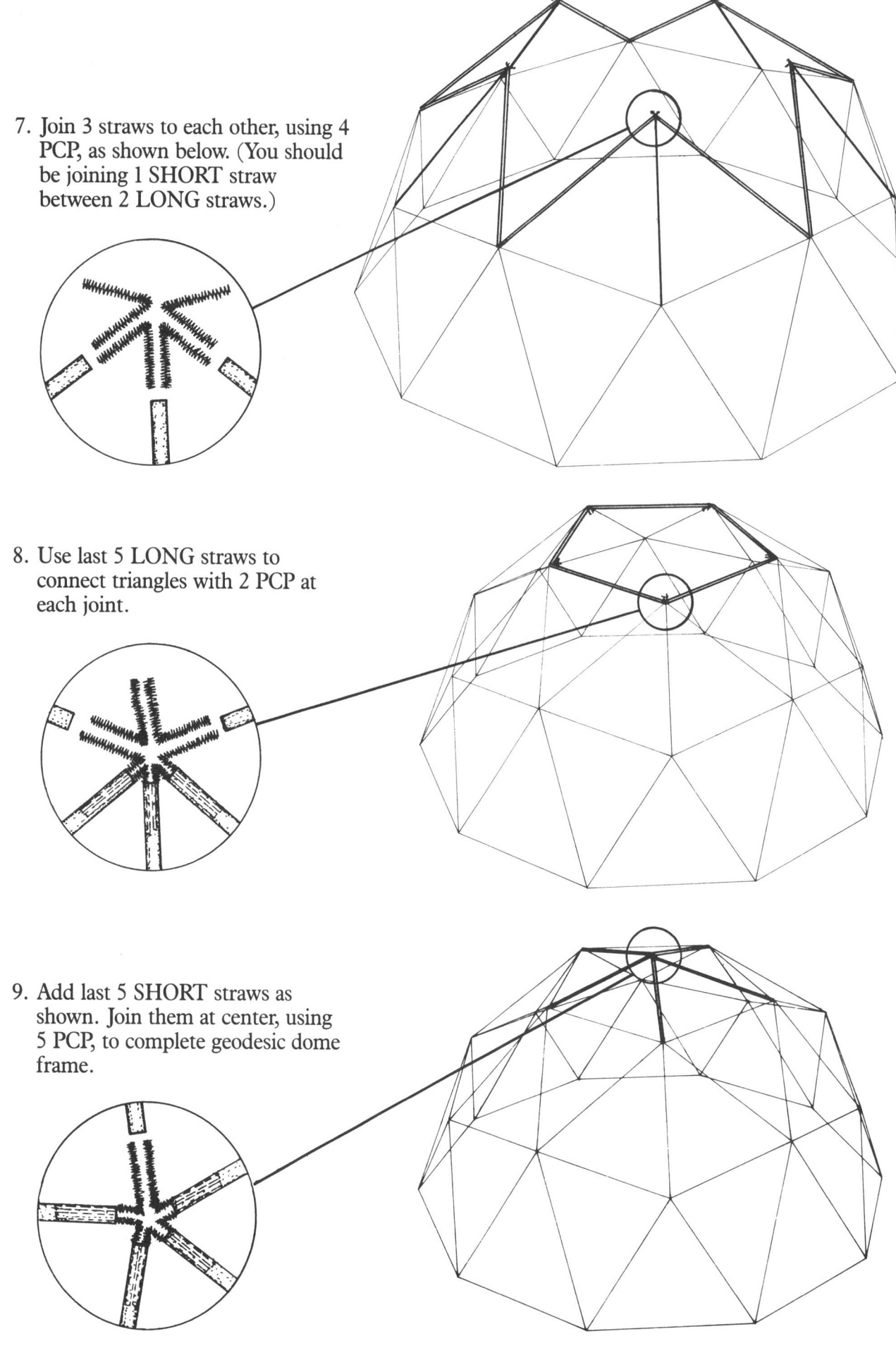

10. Trace panel patterns and transfer to cardboard or paper. 10 large panels and 30 small panels may be covered. Glue to the dome's frame. You will end up with an incredibly strong model that's light in weight and very much your own design.

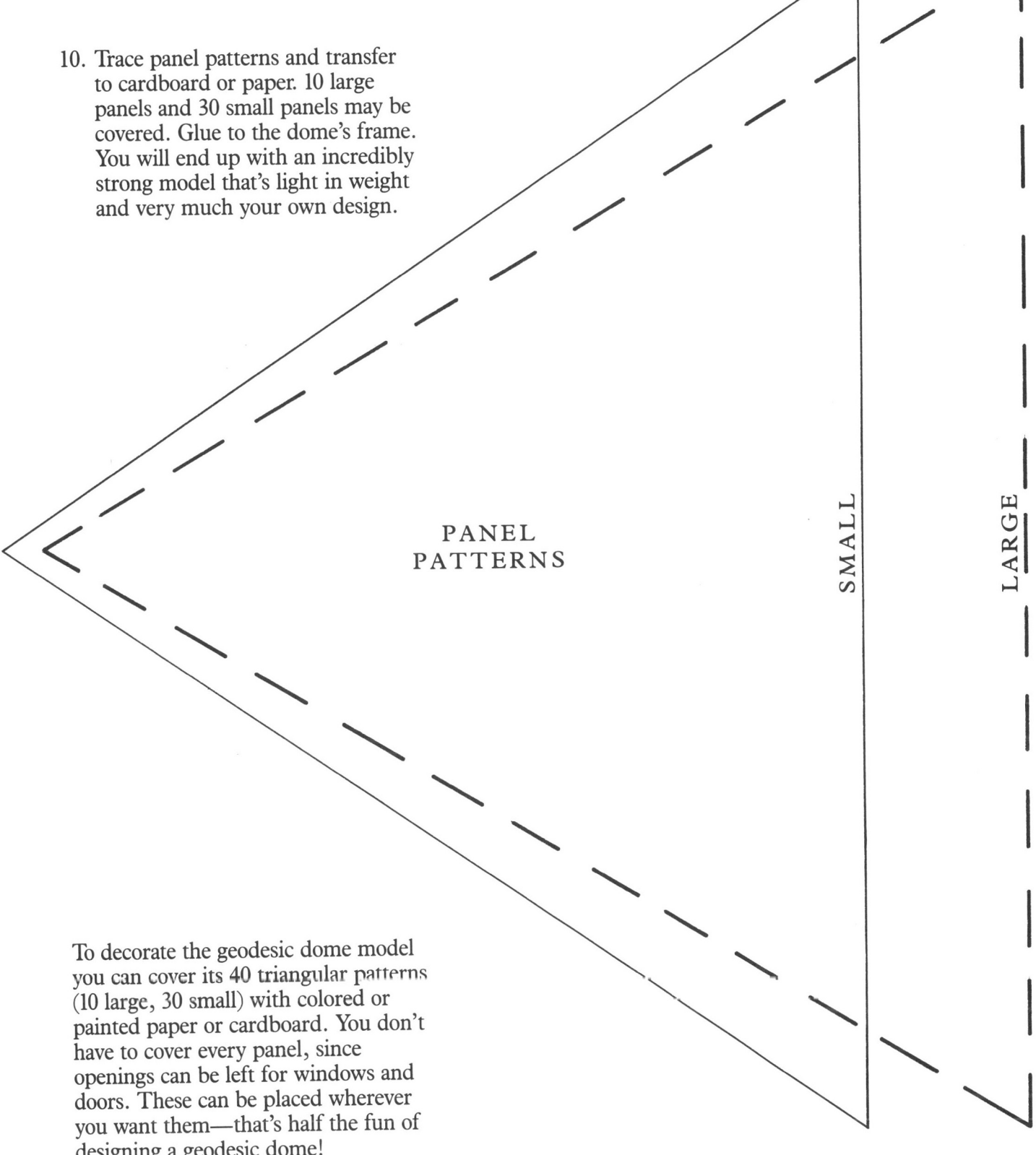

PANEL PATTERNS

SMALL

LARGE

To decorate the geodesic dome model you can cover its 40 triangular patterns (10 large, 30 small) with colored or painted paper or cardboard. You don't have to cover every panel, since openings can be left for windows and doors. These can be placed wherever you want them—that's half the fun of designing a geodesic dome!

The Future?

There is no conclusion to the dome story. Because domes make buildings special, they continue to be as popular today as they were thousands of years ago. Their shapes are not too different from what they were, though the materials they are made of certainly are.

In their earliest forms, as dwellings and tombs, they were associated with the complete life cycle. Today, they are associated with modern technology—and the future.

Domes are made of every sort of material that can be put together with a hammer and nails, and some can be inflated like a balloon. They are adaptable to different climates and locations. They are as strong as, if not stronger than, a square or rectangular building.

A clue to their past and perhaps their future may be in their name, which comes from *domus*, the Latin word for house. For this is the one structure that is basic to man. It is shelter. It is a means of survival for the family unit. For this reason domes have been important in the past. For this same reason they will play an important role in the world's future.